BROADCAST,
Bloopers & Boneheads

BROADCAST,
Bloopers & Boneheads

Behind the Scenes of Life in Media

Tamara Hinton

Copyright © Tamara Hinton
All rights reserved. No portion of this publication may be reproduced, stored in a retrieval system, or transmitted by any means—electronic, mechanical, photocopying, recording, or any other—except for brief quotations in printed reviews, without the prior written permission of the publisher.

Cover: Amy Evans and 3-Sixty Marketing Studio
Cover Design: Tamara Hinton
Editors Regina Cornell
Interior Design: Whitney Evans, SGR-P Formatting Services

Indigo River Publishing
3 West Garden Street Ste. 352
Pensacola, FL 32502
www.indigoriverpublishing.com

Ordering Information:

Quantity sales: Special discounts are available on quantity purchases by corporations, associations, and others. For details, contact the publisher at the address above. Orders by U.S. trade bookstores and wholesalers: Please contact the publisher at the address above.

Printed in the United States of America

Library of Congress Control Number: 2017964354
ISBN: 978-1-948080-09-5

First Edition

With Indigo River Publishing, you can always expect great books, strong voices, and meaningful messages. Most importantly, you'll always find…words worth reading.

To my parents Robert and Linda Hinton, whom I will always be grateful to for the solid foundation you built for me and Rotthan. I am so thankful for your constant support of my creative gifts from God. Since I was a child, that support provided me with comfort, a fearless spirit, and it pushed me creatively. Thank you for loving me.

Contents

1. Prescription drug abuse is real!   9
2. The day I found out one of my favorite ex-co-workers went to jail one night   19
3. When the news crew becomes the headline   31
4. I work at a zoo   43
5. I'm going to need an in-house internship from here on out, please!   55
6. Did the police officer ask her to sign his calendar?   65
7. Election Day   71
8. When the headline story comes to the TV station, literally   81
9. If you don't tell anybody your business, won't anybody know your business!   93
10. Why do co-worker's relationships become part of my day?   107
11. The life of TV news vehicles & equipment   117
12. Using the airwaves to get a date, while others don't go far to have an affair   127

1.
Prescription drug abuse is real!

ANOTHER DAY AT the TV news circus I call my job, and my 6 o'clock deadline is approaching. I am the evening show producer. And it is believed since I'm in a small market, that's the reason I'm the 10 o'clock producer as well. Most TV stations have one producer per show. Not here. Not only do I have the responsibility of deciding what stories will be in my newscast, what my lead story will be, write stories, and send graphic requests; now all that is normal. But, I have to edit video for my shows, make graphics, make sure every super is branded, listen to the scanner, send reporters to do their own live shot for breaking news stories, and print my scripts in a timely manner for the director. Plus, I have to make sure the reporters' stories are grammatically correct and, most importantly, factual. Oh, and pray it all goes well twice a day, five days a week. Yep! It is a lot of work and a lot of responsibility for one person. Management doesn't seem to really notice that.

So far, so good. The usual suspects are being told, "We work under a deadline; please get your work in now." I really want to say, "Dammit, I'm sick and tired of having to say every day we work under a deadline. Can you please pay attention to the time too?" I swear. I say the same thing every day to the same people. This younger generation really ain't scared of getting fired. Not even suspension without pay!

I mean! I think they come in to work under some type of influence. And if not, they do when they come back from their dinner break. For instance, the other night, I asked Jada, the Chyron operator, to make me an over-the-shoulder-graphic used on screen beside the anchor's headshot for a story about a public hearing. The hearing was held to restore the forum for residents at council meetings in Hattiesburg. A Chyron or font operator is responsible for the on-screen graphics seen on your tv. They're also responsible for popping up the name and title graphic in the lower third portion of your tv screen for people speaking during news stories. So she decides to type *Public Hearing* on the graphic she's making for my show, but instead, she typed *Pubic* Hearing. No one caught the error until after it had aired, which was too late. So of course, a viewer, who has no life, took a *screenshot* of it and posted it to the story we had up about the public hearing on Facebook. Now, it's on the Internet forever!

Even the sports' anchor, who has to get on live TV and tell sports news, will come back from his dinner break tipsy. He slurred his words on air, stumbled over words, called his highlights wrong, and inverted the final score at the end of his highlights. Really? Does he think we don't notice? Plus, we smelled the alcohol on his breath as he headed to the studio.

Aggravated to no end, it's five 'til show time and *pill-popping* Tony doesn't have the live shot up once again. So after cursing and losing all my Jesus from Sunday morning, and being loud enough to wake up a hibernating bear, his spastic ass decides, at five 'til mind you, to restart the Live U that never should have been turned back off in the first place! Before I walked into the control room, the director already had a good picture and a good mic check.

So I've had it up to here! After the newscast was over, I catch our new, fearless news director heading out the door on his way to his car and stop him to vent about Tony. I tell him how every day this week Tony hasn't had his live shot up in time, and this just ain't gonna cut it, and his ass needs to be drug tested!

I finally decided to tell him about one of the stories, there are many about Tony, from one of the reporter newbies who go out in the field with him. One night, when Savannah Rae and I were in the newsroom by ourselves, she told me about her first week on the job and her ride to a story with Tony.

She says he abruptly pulls over to the side of the road without any notice. She's nervous because it is a busy interstate where big tractor-trailers are speeding by. Now, this is her third time seeing him and talking to him since her employment at the station.

Nervously, she puts her hand on the handle to open the door, and she quickly eyes her cell phone and thinks to grab it. She may need it to make a mad dash to the nearby woods and call 911. She thought, *Really? My first TV job out of college and I'm about to become a news story. How? I'm the reporter!*

Tony manages to make it safely to the back of the news car without getting hit by a moving vehicle traveling 70 miles per hour. *What could he possibly be doing back there?* She thought.

Before she could change her mind about exiting the news car, he comes back and gets in with what looks like a medicine bag. *What is in that bag that's so important?"* she asked herself. *Is his cell phone in there?* Lord knows, I've acted erratically, damn near crazy when I realized I didn't know where my cell phone was. Now that can cause you to pull over to the side of the road suddenly, even on a busy interstate. *Could he be looking for his cigarettes?* She'd noticed how much he smoked in the short time she'd been around him. We are not supposed to smoke in company cars. She remembered reading that in what little she read of the company handbook. Maybe he got hungry all of a sudden. *Is his lunch in there? Or it could just be a snack he wanted to get until they could get lunch after the shoot. No, a gun maybe?*

She remembered from the signs in the station and on the doors outside that no guns are allowed on the grounds. Plus, we can't carry a gun in the news cars so she thought maybe he was going to put the gun in his pocket. They were on their way to cover a group of protesters mad about the county's proposal to build a new jail near their neighborhood. It crossed her mind that maybe he thought the situation would get out of hand with protestors attacking county officials and authorities. Would the protestors be that upset? We southerners do believe in the Second Amendment! We would get it tattooed on our bodies if it would all fit.

Well, her mind suddenly stopped wondering when he pulled out a bottle of pills. So, while popping pills from different bottles, Tony explained to her how he and his alcoholic girlfriend, who happened to be a pediatrician, had too much sex last night, so his back has been hurting him all day! SAY WHAT NOW? First of all, why would she want to know this, especially from someone she doesn't know?

She could only imagine what his girlfriend is like. She is a pediatrician; she has to be pretty desperate to date this *pill-head*.

She wondered how they met. Rehab? If so, obviously, it's not a good rehab. Maybe they fell in lust at first sight while out at a bar. Addicts are always enabling each other. Second, what a lie to tell someone you've known for three days when the truth is that you are a *pill-popper*.

Tony started to explain how he wasn't really in the mood, but his girlfriend kept at it until he was somewhat aroused. Wow! Is this the conversation you have with your new co-worker? He said she was "tipsy" and couldn't get her clothes off, let alone his. Shouldn't he try to help her get her clothes off? He looks lazy. Hahaha! Anyways, I'm sure she was drunk and not tipsy. As he laughed hysterically, he told Savannah Rae that he believes they managed to have sex anyways because when they woke up the next morning, they were half naked on the patio, and he hoped the neighbors hadn't seen them. *Okay enough!* She thought. *Can we just get to the story?* So, after what seemed like forever on the side of the road, Tony decided to head on to cover the story. Savannah Rae was about to get the chance to meet Tony's girlfriend. Well, sort of.

The company encourages everyone who drives company vehicles to drive safely at all times. You know, buckle up, limit cell phone use, drive the speed limit, and of course, do not drive under any kind of influence. If you are thinking like I'm thinking, the only one of those that might get done most often is buckling up.

When Tony's girlfriend called, he took advantage of the Sync system and talked to her through the car's speakers.

"Hey Savannah. The new girl Savannah Rae is in the car with me," Tony said this to cut off his girlfriend from saying something crazy with the new reporter in the car.

"Oh, you two have the same name, well she uses Rae with hers," Tony said slowly as he realized the difference.

I'm thinking the pills must be kicking in.

Then there is a pretty long pause.

So Savannah Rae jumped in and said, "Hi Savannah!"

"Hi," Savannah said.

Then she jumps right in and says, "Tony, we are having dinner tonight at my dad's and his girlfriend's. I need you there."

"I don't know if I can make it on time. I have a live shot to do for the 6 o'clock," Tony added.

"Did you not hear me say I need you there, Tony?" his girlfriend yelled.

It kind of caught Savannah Rae off guard. Tony's girlfriend's voice was really loud coming through those speakers.

"I need you there. I don't like being by myself with her and my dad. You know I don't like her ass!"

"Look Savannah," Tony yelled back. "I have to work, okay! I just can't leave and come to you whenever you want me to, woman," he said.

"Oh, I'm your woman now?" she yelled so loudly through the speakers that it left a ringing in Savannah Rae's ears.

"I was your underage cheerleader on my knees last night," she said loud and clear.

Savannah Rae was in disbelief and realized they both forgot

she was there.

"I got to go, Savannah, I'll have to call you later," Tony said and hung up.

And just like that Savannah was gone. Savannah Rae, who I've come to learn as one to never be speechless, was speechless.

"Sorry about that," Tony apologized.

Savannah Rae just sat there not knowing what to say. Luckily, they had made it to her story, and she immediately got out of the car.

So our fearless news director seems very distraught by yet another report of a dysfunctional news employee and explained to me how he is not sure what to do, but something has to be done. He says company drug tests do not pick up prescription drugs or alcoholism.

I'm thinking if the company conducted drug tests, we wouldn't have over half of our staff. I wonder sometimes if this business creates substance abusers. It is a high pressure, high performance industry where you have to be, more often than not, on your A-game. We have to come up with stories during our ratings periods. Maybe that will be my sweeps idea when we have our next meeting. Does the TV news industry create substance abusers? I'm serious! I could really have something here. Here's an idea. Have a Skype interview with Dr. Drew. Maybe Savannah Rae could do the series. Hell, she's had first-hand experience dealing with Tony.

Now, the news director goes on to tell me about the morning weatherman.

Vance called in, and said he was making repairs to his house and broke some ribs. I realized that's why Sandy had been filling in for weather on the morning show. Sandy is the weekend weather girl. I'm sure he was sloppy drunk, and that's really how he hurt himself. I've seen him sloppy drunk before at a New Year's party, and it was nothing pretty to see.

I was told last year he was so drunk at Mardi Gras in New Orleans that he flipped over a balcony and broke his back. Thank God the people below broke his fall, and he didn't kill himself. After his surgery and spending some time in the hospital, he had to be transported back here in a van where he had to lie flat all the way. Lucky for him, New Orleans is only an hour and a half drive. He was out on short-term disability for two months! Alcohol is a hell of a drug! And we seem to have an invisible sign out front saying, "substance abusers please come in and apply." We have a place for you. It is certainly entertaining to work here! It's always something. It's never ending. I'll tell you that! Well, at least tomorrow is Friday!

2.
The day I found out one of my favorite ex-co-workers went to jail one night

MOST DAYS AFTER I wake up, I do my normal routine, which includes checking my work email. If I don't check them before I get to work, I'll have a ton of emails and be behind all day. Seems like the company should have to pay me for this, right? So, immediately, I can tell what kind of day it's going to be. If I have a ton of emails, then I realize breaking news just happened with us, or at a sister station, or nationally, and the hub sent us notice that they are working on it for the web. Thank goodness I had a normal number of emails that morning. It looked like it was going to be a regular day. Who was I kidding? That could change in a heartbeat, but at least, at that moment, nothing was going on.

    I got in my vehicle and headed to work. It was such a beautiful day to have to go to work. I turned on the radio to listen to the gospel station that helps me stay in a calm and sane place. You never know what to expect once you cross the threshold of a TV station's newsroom. Sometimes, you want to stop by the liquor store first to fill-up your flask. Just kidding! No alcohol is allowed in or on company property. I would guess once it's in your body that doesn't count, huh? That must be the rule of thumb for some of my coworkers. Anywho, I park in our non-secure parking lot. I'm still shocked that nothing major has happened at the station. Viewers get upset about anything, and almost always threaten to visit the TV station. I've always told my parents to use their last dime to sue and avenge my untimely death if something ever happens to me. Well, at least the door to get in the newsroom requires a key card.

Well, as soon as I walked in, the sports girl, Heather Kirksey, yelled to our news director, "Tell Tam about Sean Lee!"

Sean, a sports reporter/anchor at the station once before, was one of several people laid off on December 10, 2008, when the company decided it was in a recession along with the rest of the U.S. Not only did they have to cut back, but people had to go. It was a sad day. I worked night side, so I didn't get to see people lose their jobs, but my phone was blowing up that whole day. Hell, I thought maybe I wasn't gonna have a job. I was told an employee would get called back and then come back to their desk to clean it out. Just like that! They were gone. Nobody got the chance to give them a proper goodbye. I heard they'd gotten rinky-dink severance packages, including Sean. But he saw a problem with his. The amount of money paid didn't match the amount of time left on his contract, along with the severance deal. See, his daddy's a lawyer, and perhaps Sean pays attention to details when it comes to contracts. So, Sean pointed this out to our news director who never, ever, liked to be wrong about absolutely anything, and surely disliked whoever pointed it out. I'm sure you know some folks like this. The news director became even more outraged because Sean was gone, and he couldn't pass by him and later talk about him behind his back. Instead, he had to correspond with Sean's lawyer from his father's law firm and comply with what they were asking. When Heather asked the news director to tell me about Sean, he was glad to do so.

He started off with a cheesy grin and got right to it, "Sean got arrested!" I was stunned!

"What did you say?" I couldn't believe my ears.

"Your boy got arrested last night," he gladly added on.

"For what?" I yelled.

"For being drunk and kicking in the door of some old man's place," he said all knowingly.

I just couldn't believe it! I know Sean can throw 'em back, I'd seen him, but I'd never seen him violent. So with a "WOW" look on my face, I took a seat at my desk. All kinds of things were running through my head. Was it really true? How could that happen? What in the hell got into him? I put in a good word to help him get that job, and now, I looked stupid.

Sean had been out of work for about six months when Rob J. and I talked one night at the station. Rob J. was the sports director at our sister station. He was tired of working so many sports stories and anchoring because they never replaced the sports guy they lost, who was Sean Vega. The news director had someone in mind from our Coast sister station, but Rob had run-ins with him before and didn't care for his work ethic or character. See, in this business, especially for TV stations in the same state owned by the same company, you tend to have to help each other out covering stories. Especially during high school football season. You can't make all the games like the public thinks you should. So when a team played another team in your sister station's area, they'd cover it and send the highlights of the game to you. Even so, when major cuts to a department happened because your multi-million dollar company thought it was in a recession, it became a matter of not enough hands on deck to be able to get work done for your own sportscast, let alone get it done for a sister station. Now, when someone, through all that adversity, pulled off their sportscast and got their sister stations needs done also, they, of course, expected the same courtesy when they needed highlights. Right? Right! Well, I think the sports guy that the news director was looking to hire for sports came up short for Rob J. on more than one occasion. You know the old adage, first time, shame on me, second time, shame on you. Plus, the candidate for hire in question never offered an apology or reason why he didn't get Rob J. the highlights although the guy got his highlights every time. And to add more fuel to the fire, the viewers were starting to call in! They would contact the sports department bitching and complaining about not seeing highlights of their team on the sportscast. That's enough to curse out the person who didn't get you the highlights, plus management who wants to consider this person for hire after you've told them the person continues to come up short. You already don't want to deal with the guy who works two markets away, so you damn sure don't want to work with him in your office. So I thought about Sean Lee and told Rob J. about him wanting to get back in the business. He had put his resume out there. Rob had dealt with Sean a few times at our station and never had a problem with him, so he was like "Tell him to call me." In the meantime, Rob J. touched base with Mitchell Williams. He's the sports director that hired Sean. Sean didn't have a perfect record, but who does? It was good enough for him to become a sports anchor/reporter once again. I was super excited for him getting back in the business. Then I started hearing some things. He got a dent in the sports car and claimed he didn't know how it got there. But a viewer called to say he backed into her parked car. His camera equipment was always banged up. Also, his coverage of the one and only Saints Super Bowl win was not up to par with management. They felt his package on the game was lackluster. That was the biggest complaint until the arrest.

I went online searching for the story about his arrest. Talk in the newsroom was that one of the competing stations in that market had the story on its website and was telling it all. I found the story. Unbelievable! I thought, *I gotta talk to him.* I had a show to do, but on my dinner break, I called him.

"Hey Tam," he said.

He wasn't as sad as I thought he should have sounded. I cut to the chase.

"What happened Sean? You got arrested?"

He said, "I did, but it's not like it sounds."

"That's not what the other station's website said. They said you were the one that kicked down the door," I pointed out.

"Well, that's not what happened, and I ought to sue their ass for getting it wrong," he said.

So I was like, "What happened then?"

He began to tell me that a bunch of co-workers decided to go out after work. He and Sean Vega had become pretty tight. Vega still lived in the area. Vega was laid off when Lee was laid off. So they knew each other and had helped each other out because of working at sister stations. Lee took the slot left by Vega's layoff in Rob J's sports department. Vega worked somewhere else and wasn't trying to get back in the business. Vega was also dating a reporter at Lee's station. Looked like to me they were dating before Vega was let go. There you go! Dating in the workplace. I told you it happens all the time. This was a good match though. They are married and now have a daughter that is Vega's twin!

The morning show's anchor's husband also went out with them including a couple of his friends. There was a production person from the station that was there too. Bottom line, everybody got too drunk. The morning show's anchor's husband, Kyle, decided he wanted to go to another friend's place who had said he was passing on the outing. Well, since it was walking distance from the bar, they paid the tab and walked to the guy's cookie-cutter apartment complex.

"Come on, you punks! Keep up," Kyle said.

Drunk as he was, he was leading the pack. Guess he should have because he knows where his friend lives. They all caught up to Kyle who had tripped and fallen and was bleeding around the knee area through his jeans.

"I got it, I don't need no help! See, I'm standing up," Kyle mumbled.

He was oblivious to the bleeding and marched on. The rest of the brood kept marching on.

"Ouch, dammit," slurred Vega.

Lee stepped on his heel.

"Sorry man, my bad," Lee slurred.

"Will y'all asses kiss and make up and come on," yelled Kyle.

"Wait up, I gotta piss," said Tommie Simon. He's a co-worker that works in sales.

Salespeople don't mix with the common news folk. But Tommie was cool. Now he is mixed up with the news crew. Ha! What a cool name, huh? Tommie Simon.

"Hell, I gotta go too," says one of Kyle's friends.

He and Tommie decided they were not going to pee outside and walked all the way back to the bar.

After the rest of the band of brothers stumble, I mean, march forward, they finally make it to Kyle's friend's apartment.

Kyle knocks on the door.

BAM! BAM! BAM! BAM! BAM! The door opens.

Kyle, all loud and crazy said, "Man, I can't believe you left us hanging brother. Why didn't you come out with us? Your ass lives just up the street." He slurred every word.

By this time, they all see a pretty girl sitting down on the couch behind the guy. The friend invited them all inside because he noticed they were all "tore up from the floor up."

"Come on in, guys," he said.

They all piled in, one behind another. They introduce

themselves to the pretty lady.

"Hi guys," she said.

So although they have disturbed his mack time, the friend realized they needed to stay put for a minute. They stayed for about 20 minutes, and Kyle decided he needed more beer and wanted to head back to the bar.

"Hey man, we are gonna get out of here," said Kyle.

"No, man, y'all ain't gotta go," the friend demands.

"Nah, bro, we're out," Kyle said as he continued to slur his words.

They all get up to leave and say their *nice to meet yous,* and they head down the walkway making a lot of noise, Kyle being the last one to leave the apartment.

Somebody's cell phone goes off and Kyle searches for his and realizes he must have left it at his friend's house. "Dammit! Where in the hell is my cell phone?" he answered his own question. "I think it's back at the apartment, shit!"

They all trekked back up the walkway behind Kyle. Lee and Vega had sobered up more than the rest and were slow getting back. Kyle began to knock on the door. No answer. He knocked harder. He thought his buddy had gone to his bedroom and couldn't hear the knocking. Still nothing. He knocked on the window a little too hard and it shattered just as an old man opened the door. Old man? They were at the wrong apartment.

Cookie-cutter apartment complex, remember? Plus, drunk, equals wrong apartment. Kyle had stumbled back to a building short of his friend's building. It was the same looking apartment, different building. Plus, the guys didn't realize all the noise they had kept up. The police had been on their way because someone called them. Well, no turning back now. The police have made it. Imagine how the scene looked to them! Back up comes quickly and the authorities began to put everyone in handcuffs. That's when another officer driving up noticed Lee and Vega down the walkway and went right ahead and handcuffed them too. The officer recognized them both from TV.

Well, there it was, guilt by association. Sean may not have kicked in the door, and now, I know who broke the window, but he was there and was drunk with his boys! The silver lining of the story is that they all survived. The state's capital city is known for being the least livable city in the state. Everybody is packing, I mean everybody. Permit or not. Crime is back at an all-time high! The fact that the old man had to be the only one in the complex without a gun is a miracle from God.

Sean would soon have no job, but he still had his life. I'm glad his folks didn't have to come I.D. his body. I'd met them before. They are really nice people. Rob J. called me later that night and fussed me out for sending him Sean. I told him I was sorry, and we laughed about how everybody at their station was talking about it and how pissed management was about it all. Plus, the icing on the cake, it was sweeps! July sweeps but sweeps nonetheless. The station was forced to publish a story, but it lacked the juicy details the competition station had. They were getting way more web hits and social media comments. It's just another day in the TV news business.

3.
When the news crew becomes the headline

WELL, IT HAD been a quiet night in the newsroom. No breaking news with thirty-four minutes to go until the newscast. I thought to myself, *print my anchor scripts for the show, and I will be done.*

At that very moment, I noticed I am missing an anchor. I have two, Jama and Steve. The show can go on with one, but I have a double anchor newscast. Now, granted, Jama is late every night getting back from her two-and-a-half hour lunch break, but this is ridiculous.

I wondered what had her running so behind. Did she get into a car accident on the way back to the station? Had she fallen asleep and awakened at the last minute at home? Did she have an extra glass of wine at dinner, maybe? Yes, your news people drink on the job all the time. Yep. It is probably that one. I think that has happened a time or two before. She had mentioned how her husband would cook dinner for her, and she would go home and eat on her break and have a glass of wine. I'm thinking, *a glass of wine?* On the rare occasion I went to hang out with some coworkers at a restaurant, I saw her drink a bottle by herself. Well, she came running into the newsroom looking crazy. She quickly touched up her makeup and hair. She didn't really say much and headed to the anchor desk. The show went well, and then, she was out the door.

When I got to work the next day, I then found out what happened.

After the morning show, the intern, who had learned how to eavesdrop very well, (trust me, you learn quickly in this business in order to stay in the know in a newsroom) overheard Gavin's phone conversation with a friend of his. Gavin was still so upset. The intern had headphones on and appeared to be editing but was listening to every word. Well, you know the rest. One person tells the next person not to tell anyone. That person tells the next person not to say a word to anyone, and that person does the same. And so on. When it is over, everyone knows what happened. Now that the story has made its way through the grapevine, I know what happened last night, and it involved Gavin.

Gavin is one of our morning news anchors and, apparently, his boyfriend locked him out of the loft they shared. He called Jama, no answer, so he texted her. Then he called Rich, one of our photographers, to help him move his things once and for all. Rich and one of our reporters, Kesha, had finished their live shot and were headed back to the station when Rich got the call, so they headed over to Gavin's. It was getting late, and Kesha hadn't had dinner and was hungry, but decided she would help Gavin out, too.

They arrived and Gavin was at the back door trying to get his key to work.

"Why won't this key work?" Gavin yells.

Rich walked up just in time.

"Hey Gavin let me see if I can get it open," Rich offered. He considered himself a pro with locks. Rich gave it a go. And another go at it. And another. "What kind of lock is this? I can break into anything," Rich bragged. They all laughed.

"Let me try," Kesha asked. Rich dropped the key. He went to pick it up and dropped the key again.

"Let me just get it butter fingers. Why are y'all acting so nervous? Let me get us in this place," Kesha said. After several attempts as well, Kesha could not manage to get the door open, either. Gavin realized Zane must have changed the lock to the front door. He thought about the back door to the laundry room. Maybe Zane didn't change that one. It was always harder to open with the key, but could be opened with a little trickery. They all walked to the back and, by this time, Jama responded to Gavin's text saying she was on her way. Gavin tried to un-lock the door and could not manage to open it. Once again, one by one, they took a turn trying to open the door.

"Stand back and let me try," Rich says.

After several tries, Kesha tells Rich, "I guess it's my turn."

After just one try from Kesha, they were in.

Jama arrived to see Gavin, Rich, and Kesha walking back and forth with armloads of items. Kesha dropped something from every other load she was carrying as Rich picked it up. Gavin's dog managed to slip out of his car at some point and was now in on the action. Jama joined in, and, after carrying her first armload of the lightest items possible, she thought to ask, "Where is Zane?"

Gavin told her, "He's out of town with his mother at a dance competition. They go to them all the time, and this is a really big one." Zane and his mom own a dance studio below the loft where he and Gavin live. Well, where Gavin used to live. As everyone continued to take out armloads of Gavin's things, he went on to say, "They are not expected back for a week. This is a regional invitation only dance completion their girls have been invited to. It is a really big deal!"

"It must be," Kesha says.

"Yeah, a whole week, that sounds pretty expensive," Rich chimes in.

"Well, there is a huge monetary first prize at stake and

bragging rights forever," Gavin explained. Jama made her way into the conversation as she dropped a box that sounded like something broke when it hit the ground.

"Zane thinks he is the male version of Abby Miller. He was told in secret there would be some producers there scoping out talent for a pilot episode for a new reality show. He thinks he and some of the girls have a shot," Jama said as she rolled her eyes.

His crazy self probably does have a chance. He's very charming and good looking, blonde, blue eyes and is about 6'2". But the odd thing I found out is that he has pectoral and calf implants. Even gorgeous people are self conscious about something. It all works to his advantage. I guess that is what attracted Gavin to him, until Zane got physical with him. Hence the reason he is packing it up and moving out! Good for him! Zane is a looker and a charmer but now is considered crazy by this group.

I'm sure you are wondering what happened. Zane got jealous of Gavin at this party because this guy was flirting with Gavin. Gavin wasn't flirting back, but that did not seem to change Zane's mind. He already thinks Gavin has this following of men because of him being a local news personality. Well, he does. But all the anchors and reporters have a big social media following. They are on air and in viewers' homes every day. Gavin is one of the first people viewers see when they wake up in the morning. Get over yourself. They got home that night and Zane had one too many, I guess, and became a bit aggressive. Gavin had never seen that side of Zane. But one time was enough for him. Whether intentional or driven by liquid courage, Zane got up in Gavin's face. Now Gavin is about 5'9" and a looker himself. He is just not as strong as Zane. Zane pushed Gavin around and then shoved him a little too hard and Gavin fell onto one of Zane's free weights that should have been in the exercise room, and bruised his face right under his left eye. We kind of noticed it at work. He was wearing more makeup than usual to cover it up, plus the area looked a little swollen. When he got under the lights, those HD cameras will show even your chicken pox scars, we could tell something did not look right. No one would say it, but we thought Gavin and Zane had a fight, and Zane hit Gavin. As you see, we were kind of wrong. So Gavin was not cool with that and, unknown to us, he was staying at a friend's house and not answering Zane's calls. So Zane changed the lock. Gavin knew Zane would be out of town so he figured he would go move out, but didn't know he had been locked out.

So as everyone continued to help Gavin get his things out of the house, Jama realized what the scene must have looked like.

"You guys do realize we look like a bunch of thieves, right?" she said. Everybody started to laugh in agreement.

"Well, maybe they will see the station logo on my vehicle and just think we are working," Rich said.

Kesha said, "Really, Rich? None of us has a mic in our hand. Just armloads of these expensive items of Gavin's." Everybody laughed at what Kesha said but thought about how she was right. They had carried out Gavin's artwork, including an original watercolor of Lady Gaga that looked pretty impressive. They had removed his enormous wardrobe of tailored suits and handmade Italian shoes, not to mention his casual clothes. Rich thought to himself, *How much is he getting paid?* He helped carry out a full length, ginormous, ornate floor mirror that was absolutely gorgeous! Jama shared her concern of what would happen if the police drove by with the group hauling out all of this stuff. This wasn't just a residence, but a business as well. Tony pulled up, scaring the crap out of everybody before they realized it was him. Apparently, Gavin had more stuff than he realized and called Tony for backup. So now Gavin and Jama's cars were jammed packed with Gavin's stuff, as was Rich's station vehicle. Tony joined in to load up his company vehicle as everyone continued to carry out the last items of Gavin's from the loft and dance studio. Tony, who often complains of back problems, grabbed some sofa pillows, while Kesha dragged what looked like an expensive floor vase. Gavin may have been better off hiring some movers.

Well, Jama, being from Miami, must have smelled the cop

from miles away because here he came with a big, bright, flood light from his car. No siren. The crew hadn't noticed him just yet. He stopped because he saw the two station vehicles and thought we were filming something going on that he didn't know about. Something was going on all right. The officer hadn't heard any police chatter. As he got out of his patrol car and came closer with his bright flashlight, he saw every vehicle, including the TV station vehicles, packed full of stuff. Plus, he noticed no one else is around but the TV people with all this stuff packed up along with items in their hands. Tony walked out with yet another piece of Gavin's art in his hand. He loudly commented on the original photograph he recognized.

"Gavin, do you realize how much this photograph is worth?" Tony said.

Without noticing the police officer, nor giving Gavin time to respond, Tony said, "You could get thousands of dollars for this!" Tony looked up and saw the police officer and realized they were caught red handed! The rest of the crew now noticed him, too. The officer asked, "What is going on?" Obviously, he knew who everyone was from TV, but was confused.

They began to explain, but of course didn't include that the lock was changed and that they had to break in through the back door. By this time, another officer arrived on the scene because he got a call about a breaking and entering incident at this address.

Apparently, one of Zane's messy friends who knew about the break up, and Gavin staying with another friend, and Zane changing the lock, called Zane after he passed by the dance studio. Zane called the police, and there you go. Both cops recognized everybody involved and were not clear about the current situation. So they told everyone they're going to have to come down to the station to sort all this out. They all left with one cop car in the front and one cop car in the back, with the news vehicles and Gavin and Jama's cars in the middle. I bet that was a sight to see.

They all made it to the police station and were questioned one at a time in a private area, each telling their version of how they became a part of the *help-Gavin-escape-his-abusive-lover* plan. After testimony from a good chunk of our news staff, officers decided that it was what it was, Gavin moving out his things from where he used to live after breaking up with his boyfriend. Plus, Gavin had a key that fit one of the doors. It didn't hurt that they all worked at the news station and had to be telling the truth. Working at a TV station has its perks, I guess. Everyone was free to go.

So that's how Jama almost missed the 10 p.m. newscast. What a story. At least no other media outlet made it to the scene. It was just breaking and entering. They probably heard it on the scanner and decided the next day they would just check the jail docket for the report. It wasn't worth rushing to film. If they only knew that it was photographers, reporters, and anchors from the rival news outlet as the news story that would have made their headlines for sure. Their social media pages would have gotten so many hits and shares; it would have been so good for them, and so embarrassing for us. All involved would have been in a meeting. No telling what management would have done!

Luckily for them, the news people didn't become the news story of the day. This incident would have been the talk of the town. Viewers love gossip. Well, let me say people love gossip, especially when it involves news personalities and their personal lives. This story would have been talked about for days, weeks, and months to come.

I wouldn't be surprised if management finds out. The way it spread around the newsroom and, trust me, somebody in law enforcement is going to tell the next shift about what happened. It could be the dispatcher at the police station or the janitor cleaning up, to a trustee going about the jail. Oh, somebody saw that they were not covering a story but being questioned for something. Everybody knows somebody, and it will come full circle back to management. Eventually.

Plus, the intern said he saw a picture on somebody's cell phone where these jokers took a photo together behind bars for the hell of it.

Broadcast, Bloopers & Boneheads

What the public doesn't know about their news personalities won't hurt them!

4.
I work at a zoo

I WORK AT a zoo, literally and figuratively. Hold on, and I will explain. Our station is located in the county. We have to drive several miles just to go get something to eat, unless you want something from Mak's gas station or the Dollar General up the street. The property is surrounded by a lot of dense trees. Plus a railroad track behind us that is in use. You can hear the train whistle blow on your TV when it passes through while we are broadcasting. There have been many instances when something outside the station has tried to get inside the station. Some have been successful. One night, between my 6 and 10 p.m. shows, my director Wilhemina decided to go back to the engineering department to find Ricky D. She was looking for him to ask him how to fix a piece of equipment at her church. She directs the Sunday morning service. Ricky D. can fix anything and doesn't mind coming to help you out! Plus, he fixes it on the first try and doesn't talk about you behind your back to others because you don't know technical stuff. Heck, anybody can learn and know how to do it once you've shown them, and they do it! Before him, you hated to call on an engineer. It was as if you were bothering them. Crazy right? Mina found out what she needed to know from Ricky D. and headed back to the control room to wait for show time. She didn't make it to the control room as quickly as she thought she would. Mina was stopped dead in her tracks by a visitor that made it to the inside of our building without going through the receptionist to check in. She's not here anyways because it's after hours, but I'm just saying. A snake about 5 feet long, and unidentifiable by Mina, crossed the path in front of her. Her scream was so loud that the snake hid under a piece of equipment and the master control operator ran out of his area to her aid. Once she was safe, Mina that is, somebody called Race. Race is the grandson of one of our photographers, Eddie Robertson. Race is also a studio camera operator and our own Crocodile Dundee. He comes to save the day. Well, night. This is when I found out what had been going on over on the other side of the building. Now, I was hard at work building a newscast. TV news producers are the hardest working people in the building, by the way. I'm interrupted by the ruckus from the gang of monkeys in a zoo, a.k.a the night crew, and forced to look up to see a line following behind Race through the newsroom. He's carrying a black cage with the outsider that made it in as the star attraction in one hand, and what looks like a stick in the other hand.

"Race? What in the hell is this? Aren't you off tonight?" I asked.

"Yes, I am, but Mina found a snake, well, it found her and I came to get it," Race replied.

"Oh, I see," I said.

I bet that was a sight to see! I'm sure management will be getting a nice little email from her. Yep! I'm positive they will.

"So, what are you about to do with it?" I asked.

"Oh, I'm about to take it to the woods and release it."

"What? It's a snake! Kill it!" I demanded.

"Tam it's not poisonous."

"Uh, I don't care about that! Kill it!" I said.

"Tam, calm down. These kinds of snakes eat rodents, like rats," Race explained.

Oh, I thought. That may be okay. Sticky pads had been placed on the floor in quite a few places by engineering to catch the growing number of them around the station. Matter of fact, Race ran across one on a sticky pad in the lounge one day. Yes, he released it so it could go tell others from his clan about the new place he had found to feast. Race was so mad about it. He said it was inhumane. Huh? He sent out a long email to all employees about how this wasn't right. How would you like to be caught on a sticky pad and left to die? He went on and on making his point. The email was so good that I read the whole thing. I had a good laugh although it was no laughing matter to Race. Our general manager sent out an email asking folks to bring issues to him, and not send out a mass email. Apparently, when we send out mass emails, corporate gets them too. Hell, maybe they would put some extra money in the budget for pest control.

Race left and the tribe of monkeys quieted down after the excitement. I'm sure Mr. Snake has gone on to pass along his DNA to many other rodent eating snakes. Another day Race came to the rescue once again. This time Reagan, Race's uncle, came, too.

I got to work one day, and I couldn't get to my desk good before everyone at one time wants to tell me about the alligator Race and Reagan wrestled out of the station's lagoon out back. What? Eddie takes the lead on the storytelling since these are his folks that flexed their muscle to save us from the people-eating gator.

A couple of engineers and the sports guys, along with some photographers, were letting off some steam out back, hitting golf balls. We have a massive backyard that engineers keep cleared with our station's riding lawn mower. We still have a grounds crew that keeps the bushes and flowers pretty and the plants watered, but it was cheaper to get our own riding lawn mower because the grass grows so fast. Do you think it has something to do with the lagoon? Daniel, Austin, and Jonathan were hitting their balls the farthest to the trees. Hence, they are the sports guys. Chief engineer, Mr. Clyde, wasn't coming too far behind. John Brown, one of our reporters, was running neck and neck with the sports guys. He's a former college football player and still fit, so he's knocking them over the trees. He decides to go collect some of his balls. His stash was getting low. That's when he spots "The Gator in the Goon."

"Tam! We couldn't believe it," Eddie says. When I got back there, I called Race. Reagan was with him, so he came along, too, and brought a cage with him."

Where do they get all these animal cages? I'm thinking.

"He was pretty big!" Eddie goes on to say.

"Not the biggest we've seen, though," He makes clear.

"They wrestled the gator and roped his mouth shut, Tam. You should have seen it!"

They took pictures and selfies and later drove to a wooded area and released the gator into the woods. Wow! What a day! Why do I continue to think situations can't be topped around here?

So, of course, the web team sees this as an opportunity for web hits and Facebook shares and turns the gator's human invasion into a news story. And, like clockwork, the web hits, Facebook shares and likes came flooding in. What's about to happen next, no one anticipated. We are in South Mississippi.

This kind of story attracts a multitude. The comments come fast by the dozens. From "I've seen bigger." To pictures pointing out "look at the one I caught." To "it's not gator season." Did you call the Mississippi Department of Wildlife, Fisheries and Parks? Uh oh! Apparently, there's a little law out there that says, outside of gator season, you have to call out the professionals when you run across a gator. Well, good ol' social media gives you the exposure you want and don't want, and now, Wildlife, Fisheries, and Parks pays us a visit. Luckily for us, they were somewhat lenient. There is a huge fine associated with moving a gator this time of year, but since they didn't harm the gator in any way, or kill it, the fine was significantly reduced. Plus, I think Eddie knew someone who worked there. No good deed goes unpunished. Oh, the adversity of social media.

Now, I have my own story to tell. I noticed one week, after I parked, several holes were dug up outback where we hit golf balls. I've hit several. Didn't realize I have a good swing until the guys saw me hit. Luck, I guess, because golf is not my thing. I'd rather drive around in the cart. I'm thinking, *Is somebody digging up our balls? Is it that serious?* The holes looked mighty deep. I get inside the station and get settled in. Then I head back to engineering. I find Ricky D.

"Hey, Ricky D!" I said.

"Hey, Tam, what's up?" he replied.

"Are you guys digging up all those holes looking for golf balls out back?" I asked.

"Nope!"

"Well, who is?"

"A pack of wild boars," he explained.

"What?"

"They came out of those woods looking for food and dug out holes in the ground."

"It must be something pretty good in the ground because there's some pretty big holes out there."

"Yep!" he said.

"Alright, then, see you later."

The next day, I get to work and park, not even thinking about what happened yesterday. I cut my vehicle off and get out. I grab my lunch and MacBook Pro and pull out my key card. By this time, I noticed something in my peripheral vision. I looked and focused, and something looked back and focused on me. I'd never seen a wild boar, despite being from Mississippi and working at a TV station located in rural Mississippi. But it was pretty easy to figure out that this is what a wild boar looks like! I was frozen. It was frozen. Who was going to make the first move? That would be me, for the door. I got hot and panicky real quick although it was already 97 degrees with the heat index. I was inside so fast without looking back. I made it in on the other side of the steel door that's been there since the station first went to air in 1956. I figured he would have a time getting through that. I put my things down on the counter behind the weather office and let my curiosity get the best of me. I slowly opened the door, looking down, and I saw nothing. I opened the door wider and still nothing. I looked up and over the satellites and saw the boar digging up the ground. I guess he wasn't bothered by my interrupting him and was just happy to find food to eat. I closed the door and left the outside zoo to enter into the zoo on the inside of the newsroom.

I had an encounter some years back with an outsider where I didn't wind up so lucky, but I did survive. Thank God!

I was bitten by a brown recluse spider at work. Shocked? Yes, you and me both. This happened in the youth of my TV career. I was a production assistant. I was almost at the bottom of the barrel. It was a promotion up from the studio camera operator I had been. Plus, it was full time. I needed the insurance because, back then, I was emancipated from my parents' insurance once I graduated from college. I was working one weekend editing the curse words out of an old movie we would eventually air to fill a programming slot that we couldn't sell. Now, remember, this was many, many, moons ago. The late 90's. I was editing tape. I believe it was three quarter inch tape. Yep! I just lost a bunch of you. Imagine a big VCR tape. Okay, some of you now remain lost. Anyways, it was a format used to play movies on, like today's DVD. Now, we're all on the same page. I was in my office by myself minding my own business when I noticed a spider crawl underneath from where my feet were. I immediately screamed and put me feet up in the chair I was sitting in. The Master Control operator came running to my aid.

"Are you alright Tam?" Jay asked.

"I am," as I pointed to the spider still crawling across the floor.

He stepped on it and killed all its ambitions to strike again. I hadn't realized it had bitten me. I thanked him for saving me and went back to work so did he. The next morning, I woke up at my parent's house. I'm full time but that doesn't mean I can afford my own place yet. I tell my mommy about how my foot won't stop itching. She makes a joke that I need to wash it. We both laugh. A little later, my foot begins to feel tight. Then it starts to swell. I have a born and raised Southern mother who uses Epsom Salt to cure everything. So this situation was no different. I began to soak my foot and, at first, I did get some relief, but, eventually, my foot started to tighten and swell more. Off to immediate care we went. I get back to see the doctor.

She examined my foot and says, "It looks like something bit you. Do you remember getting bit?"

I told her, "No, I don't remember feeling anything biting me."

Then I thought about last night. "Wait a minute! A spider crawled out from under the spot I was sitting in last night at work, but I didn't feel anything bite me."

"Sometimes you don't feel it," she says. "What did it look like? Was it about the size of a quarter, you think?" as she looks in between my big toe and the next toe.

"Yeah, I believe it was! I didn't have a hard time spotting it. It wasn't bigger than that, and it was brown," I remembered.

"Ok. It looks like you were bitten by a brown recluse spider. I see some peeling here."

"Oh my gosh! We ran a story last week about a Memphis baby dying from a brown recluse bite. I work at a TV station," I explained.

I'm hysterical!

"Am I going to die? Please get me to the emergency room!"

"Well, I don't think you are going to die, but this is serious," she said. "Have you had a tetanus shot before?"

"I don't think so. I absolutely do not like shots, so I would have remembered that," I said as a tear falls down my face.

By this time, I'm asking for my mommy as they prepare for my tetanus shot. My mom comes and holds my hand. I squeeze the life out of hers almost. Did I mention I've NEVER liked shots?

"I'm going to stick you in your arm, and it is going to hurt a little bit," the doctor explained after I got a glimpse of the really big needle and felt like I was going to faint.

It was over, and tears and snot were everywhere. And, slowly, I forgot that I could lose my foot and focused on the fact that my arm felt like it was about to disconnect from my shoulder. I was miserable. The doctor put some kind of medicine on my foot, wrapped it up, and told me I would have to come see her three times a week for her to check on the wound, treat it, and bandage it back up. I got crutches, too, and a doctor's excuse to stay off my foot. I told those jokers at work what happened and the HR lady at the time questioned my story. Huh? That dusty-ass place is filled with spiders, snakes, and rats. I had to get Jay, the master control operator, to back me up, and tell that heifer what happened.

What if I had never seen the spider? Nor had Jay to be a witness? They were satisfied with his account, but they didn't do me right. It should have been workman's comp, but they made me use my sick days. I think I still had all of them. When you are young and new to the full-time work force, you are eager to work and come to work sick. How wrong of them not to look out for me when I didn't know. They should have paid for my doctor's visits too, and not my insurance. I realize I'm still upset about that. College graduates, read your handbook. Be better than me!

New employees were not excluded from run-ins from

outsiders. One weekend, the new sports girl, Carrie Anderson, was in a hurry to get to a sports story. She hadn't been to the place before, so she wanted to leave a little early. She opens the door to leave and an emu was staring her right in the face like *what?* She was stunned, and late to her story. Unbeknownst to us, there was an emu farm nearby and the thing had escaped.

New reporter, Dawn Russell, had already had a pretty tough first week. She goes out in a canoe with her photographer, Jacob, to do what she knew would be a kick ass stand-up, and he turns the canoe over. Week two, she goes to use the restroom next to the sports office, and is actually using it, when a snake comes through the bottom of the wall from the sports department. She handled it really well. Better than me. Everyone would have seen drawers and all with me. She didn't scream or anything. She just came and told us about it so someone could go in there and get it and release it. What is it with releasing snakes? Kill 'em!

Did I mention I work in a zoo?

5.
I'm going to need an in-house internship from here on out, please!

I WOKE UP today to two separate manhunt push-alert notifications from the station on my cell phone. Why on a Monday? People usually wait toward the end of the week, and weekends especially, to break the law.

I was praying on my way to work that by the time I got to my desk, authorities would have used their stun guns on the two suspects and placed them in jail! I make it to work and half of my plea had come true.

As I sit in my chair at my desk, Rusty gets off his cell phone to come tell us, "They got him." Those authorities earned their paycheck. They caught their suspect and will be home before nightfall.

"The other guy, they can't seem to catch," Rusty added.

I quickly realized my lead story would be, you guessed it, the manhunt. Apparently, this joker kept slipping through the hands of authorities. He had managed to steal three cars, and abandoned all of them, and was now on foot in the woods he knows all too well. Prior to that, the sheriff said he kidnapped his now former girlfriend, who managed to escape after the suspect stopped at his house to get a hit of meth before he continued his journey. Well, it quickly became clear that he is the only one who knows the wooded area since the forty plus officers from various law enforcement agencies, fully armed with guns cocked and loaded and wearing bulletproof vests, I might add, can't capture him.

Terrica our assignment editor, decided to send the new intern with Rusty.

"Hey, Rusty," she called out.

"Yeah." Rusty replied as he hung up his phone and walked over to her.

"I'm going to send the intern with you on this manhunt, ok?" she told him.

"Alright, I just hope he can keep up, because I think this is going to be a good one," he said as he chuckled. Rusty loved going on stories like this. He is buddies with most of those law enforcement guys. His dad was in law enforcement. Had been for years. I think he works in the D.A.'s office now. Although he didn't follow in his dad's footsteps, Rusty is involved with law enforcement just about every day.

So, Rusty, our fearless crime reporter, along with the new intern, Reed, cover the story. Wow! What a sweet gig for the new intern. I was pretty sure he had never seen action like that. He has only had assignments here in the newsroom. Reed is good at writing for the web. He quickly caught on to the software we use to put stories onto our website. I asked him to be on a camera for my newsroom hit in my newscast one day, and he said he could do it. I asked him because the guys on the clock found everything else to do to avoid being on camera for my show. I was skeptical about him doing it because I needed him to shoot it with the camera off the shoulder. These jokers around here who get paid can't get the shot right half the time. Show time comes, and he killed it! This kid can do no wrong. He has nailed everything I have asked him to do. Reed is the best intern ever!

"Hey, Reed?" Rusty called out to the intern.

"Yeah," he replied.

"You want to go on this manhunt with me?" Rusty asked.

Reed jumped up and said, "I sure do! Do I need to load up the gear?" he asked.

"Sure you can. I'll make a call to see where everyone is now, so we will have an idea where in the woods to go," Rusty said. He made the call as Reed went back and forth to the news car with their gear. You could see the excitement on his face. I don't think he realized what he was in for. It is a manhunt, not a video game.

The guns will be real, and the bullets they fire will be too!

The location of the manhunt is pretty remote. Reed used his GPS to get them where they are now, but these countryside roads with no address do not show up. Rusty pulled over and called one of his law enforcement buddies in the manhunt.

"Man, where in the hell are y'all?" he asked.

"Un huh, uhhh... yeah... yeah, ok!" Reed heard Rusty say as Rusty whipped the car around, tires spinning and all, shifting the equipment around in the back. I guess this is how they are always breaking the equipment and sending it to engineering when they get back with a blank look on their face that says *I don't know how it got broken*. Obviously, they had gotten close because shortly Reed saw the officers with rifles in hand. Shit just got real for him! His heart started beating fast while Rusty stopped the car. He got out and went for the equipment. Rusty got out of the car like the cavalry had just arrived, and now, things can pop off. He shook hands with the sheriff and the rest of the guys he knew, which was just about everybody. Reed made it over and Rusty introduced him to everyone.

"What's the deal now, sheriff?" Rusty asked.

"Well, son, we got him somewhere between over there and there," the sheriff pointed. "But when I send my boys in to surround this motherfucker, he slips away, Goddammit!!! We got to get his ass," the sheriff reiterated. "My grandson is in something at the church tonight, and my wife said my ass better be there this time. I had to call in some help," the sheriff admitted.

The sheriff explained that after hours of not being able to catch this guy, he decided to call one of his deputies out on vacation in to work. That had to suck for the deputy, but he knows the area blindfolded. How crazy is that? Dozens of officers can't catch this guy, and now, one officer is about to get the job done. Having a wooded area as your playground as a child ain't so bad after all. Looks like somebody is about to get a promotion.

Rusty phoned in to let us know the suspect may be in custody by show time. Dammit! I already had in my head how I wanted my show to go. My open intro is written, and I have written what I want my anchors to say about this manhunt. I wanted the suspect caught after the 6 p.m. show was over! To try and to get all of my production people involved to switch gears quickly about a last-minute change is like telling a pregnant woman who needs to get to the hospital that the cab driver didn't stop at the hospital she wants, and to hold it in until they get to the right hospital. Her water is going to break all over the back seat or the baby could just go ahead and pop out! What I'm trying to say is my crew will hear me, but won't punch the right buttons and just do their own thing! Basically, something I want to happen will not make it to air. Oh, the anxiety!

So while I anticipated, all hell to break loose, I found out our fearless journalist, Rusty, had managed to get him and intern Reed bulletproof vests! The sheriff felt if the two of them were going to be that up close to the manhunt with a camera, they needed to have vests on too. How cool is that? It beats sitting behind a desk, writing from news releases all the time.

So the sheriff's deputy that knows the area arrived and authorities reinforced the perimeter. They know the suspect is still holding out in the wooded area. Now, the suspect can't escape.

"Gather around and listen up everybody," the sheriff yelled.

"Sheriff Deputy Nathan Robertson is here with us and is about to explain what is about to happen, Nathan," the sheriff said as he motioned for the deputy to take center stage.

"Everyone, it has been a long day for y'all already, but it is about to be over," Deputy Robertson assured everyone.

He went on to explain how they would execute and surround the suspect and, hopefully, apprehend him alive, but they are going in with guns cocked and ready to shoot to kill. No one knew if the suspect was armed. They only had to go in three directions because there is a creek behind him, the deputy tells everyone.

All law enforcement there began to double-check their guns and ammo. Reed noticed a dog had now arrived with his trainer. Reed overheard the officer saying once the suspect was found without a firearm, Kilo, the officer's dog, who is apparently a well-trained assassin, would go in for the kill. Well, the take-down. The officers were all in agreement that there is a good chance the suspect would try to run.

It is now show time. Armed officers, Kilo, Rusty and intern Reed all start to enter into the wooded area from three sides. Of course Rusty is with the side that has Kilo because he assumes that is where most of the action would be. Everyone is trucking though the brush and the soggy ground. Reed is behind Rusty and is wedged in between him and the officer behind him. His mind begins to race, and he hopes the officer raises his gun up high enough in case he has to shoot the suspect. His stomach starts churning.

Kilo got anxious because the suspect was close. Earlier, Kilo had sniffed out the abandoned cars and now knew the suspect's scent. Kilo's trainer unleashed him. And action! Kilo got out front and everybody chased behind him. Rusty had his gear and ran with it in his hand. Reed was running as well with that heavy bulletproof vest on that seemed to be weighing him down. Officers are yelling commands to one another while Kilo barked wildly and soon started to growl. The suspect, now in the grip of Kilo, yelled out in agonizing pain. By the time the officers got close enough to see what was going on, the suspect was waving around a stick that authorities identified from a distance…you guessed it, as a firearm. Everyone was yelling, and hollering, the officers, the suspect, Kilo.

"Put down your weapon," authorities yelled at the suspect.

He did not, because the pain of Kilo's grip would not let him stop beating at the well-trained dog. Authorities fired shots into the air, and Reed threw up! The suspect finally dropped what was thought to be a firearm. Officers drew closer and handcuffed the suspect. It was all over. And it was over before my show started, but I wasn't bent out of shape because it was in enough time to make changes to a show that no one had looked over yet. My newscast went well. Rusty did a live shot and an interview with the sheriff who gave a breakdown of how the day went as well as the capture.

I headed back to the newsroom, and I see Rusty and Reed made it back to the station. Rusty looked fine, but I noticed Reed didn't look well. As he walked around to the bathroom, I noticed he still had on his bulletproof vest! Hmmm… Rusty started to laugh and started to tell us how the day was a bit too much for Reed.

According to Rusty, Reed had done well until the action to capture the suspect began. Rusty said he noticed Reed was lagging behind, but he caught up with everyone soon. Then the scene became intense and that is when he saw the intern vomit on himself and drop to the ground on his knees. Rusty said he continued recording the capture of the suspect. He couldn't miss the best part by trying to help the intern. We were all bent over laughing. Rusty believed Reed peed on himself but gave him the benefit of the doubt because, luckily, it had been a wet day. By this time, there was not a dry eye among us. I hurt myself laughing so hard but managed to ask why Reed still had his bulletproof vest on. Rusty explained the sheriff didn't really want his vest back with vomit on it and suggested Reed clean it up best he could and bring it to the sheriff's office tomorrow. It looked like intern Reed was about to renegotiate his internship. Wow! It was just Monday.

6.
Did the police officer ask her to sign his calendar?

IT IS STARTING out to be somewhat of a slow news day. Around here, though, that can change in a heartbeat. The news gods decided to throw us a bone. We get a news release about one of the police departments getting a couple of K9s to add to its drug task force. Coco and Caine. Yep! Cocaine is a hell of a drug! Coco and Caine have been trained to take it off the streets. So, Terrica decides to send Bailey to cover the story since she's been sitting around all morning with no story. She is relatively new. She had called the people she's met so far. No luck. A lot of the time, folks are waiting for a friendly face or phone call to spill the beans to. Well, now, she has a story and is on her way, and my story count goes up by one.

Bailey returns with her story on Coco and Caine, but she is looking a little strange and comes to talk to Terrica and me.

Let me take a second to give you some background on Bailey. Before she got into the TV news business, she was a Saintsation! "Who Dat Talkin Bout Beatin Dem Saints? Who Dat? Who

Dat?" Well, she had to quit due to a news personality clause in her new TV news contract. What a bummer right? But before she put that on her resume because she said she was told that would be a resume booster, she'd done all the promotional publicity stuff, online spread, media packet, promos, commercials, promotional events, and, last but not least, the Saintsation calendar. So, now, all that is out in the universe for everyone to see. And, sooner than later, it gets out that the new girl at the TV station is a Saintsation. The public doesn't understand "was" a Saintsation because the season just started, and she is in the calendar.

Bailey began to explain to us that when she arrived to do her story at the police department, the public information officer was nowhere to be found. The secretary made a phone call, and the P.I.O. finally arrived twenty minutes later without the dogs. Fifteen minutes later, they arrive with their trainer. Aggravated from having to make small talk with the P.I.O. officer, she began to set up and do her interview with Coco and Caine's trainer. It went well. She even cheered up after getting the chance to pet the dogs. I wouldn't have wanted to pet them. Coco and Caine sound like killers to me! Now, if she can hurry through the P.I.O.'s interview, she'd be done. She finished up, and he actually helped her take her equipment out to her news car. After handing her the last piece of equipment, Bailey turned around, and the

Broadcast, Bloopers & Boneheads

P.I.O., with a Saintsation's calendar in hand, opened up, asked her if she knew the girl on the calendar.

Bailey said, "Yes. She's Kriste Lewis, the local woman I interviewed who made history by making the Saintsations at forty years old."

So, at that point, Bailey knew what was coming next.

The P.I.O. flips the calendar to December and asked, "Is this you?"

Bailey said, "Yes."

Terrica and I are cracking up laughing by now. Bailey told us the P.I.O then asked her, with Sharpie in hand, to sign it! We lost it! Did the police officer really ask her to sign his calendar? While he is at work and she is, too?

So I had to ask, "Did you sign it, Bailey?"

She started to laugh, too, and said, "Yes!"

Ahhh! Hilarious! Poor Bailey. What a day! Could he have not waited to possibly see her out socially and asked her to sign his calendar? I guess not.

Just last week, she had to deal with her own co-worker. Tony called her over to his desk to show her what he had edited for her sweeps piece so far, and she saw that her Saintsation's December calendar pose is his screen saver! Really? She was livid and went to HR. HR told her to tell the news director as well, so she did. All management did was make Tony write her a letter. He did so with a two sentence vague apology.

Behind the scenes in the news business is definitely entertaining! Especially for the on-air talent. They get recognized in public places all the time. That is normal, I guess, since they are in folks' homes every day. It is one thing to be recognized and another thing to be expected to engage when relaxing at dinner or while you are shopping for groceries. They tell me how this happens to them all the time. My anchor, Karrie, says she goes in the grocery store with a hoodie on. It works for her. I've had the chance to see how the public reacts to the on-air talent firsthand. Karrie's approach didn't quite work for Ontario.

Ontario and I decided to go to a Southern Miss game. It's both of our alma mater. She decided to dress down and wanted me too, as well. We are southern belles. We go everywhere "beat!" I agreed and rocked a sportier look. She puts on a baseball cap.

"Girl I am not wearing a baseball cap," I said firmly. "My hair stylist, Michael Jefferson, has slayed this hair today, honey!"

"You don't have to, but I do so that we can enjoy the game. You know folks recognize me," she said. "When I wear this baseball cap, people keep going," she added.

We head to The Rock. We can't find a parking spot anywhere close. Ontario took a wrong turn and ended up at the paying alumni parking area. The attendant saw we did not have the proper sticker, I guess, plastered somewhere on the windshield and told us we could not park there.

"There is open parking available over there," he said as he pointed in that direction.

"Oh, hey! You are the news lady on TV, he said.

So much for the baseball cap, huh?

"Yes, I am," Ontario responded.

"Well, listen, I'm going to go ahead and let you in," he said. "Just don't park up close over there, park back this way. This parking area never fills up all the way. Nobody won't even notice one more car," he finished saying.

"Thank you so much!" Ontario said.

We drove right on through and parked.

"Girl, the cap ain't working, but that's a good thing. It is too hot to have walked all that way," I said.

"I know, right? He was nice to let us in. I guess being recognized sometimes ain't so bad, huh?"

We both laughed.

"Today? Definitely not," I added.

Obviously, being recognized from TV news has its' perks sometimes. Until you do that controversial story that everyone has an opinion about and wants to tell you theirs when they spot you. That's what happened the next week at work for Ontario. She needed more than a baseball cap that week. I think she took a page from Karrie's book and wore a hoodie.

7.
Election day

THE NESHOBA COUNTY Fair, Mississippi's giant house party, has ended. A good time had by all. Some saw Mary holding baby Jesus after one too many in the Mississippi summer heat, just before the dog days set in, and right before we reach a triple heat index. Why in the world would people meet up at over one-hundred-fifteen-year old cabins, passed down through their families from one generation to the next, in these conditions? The upcoming primary elections! Every red vote, from Tunica County, to Harrison County and all points in-between want to hobknob with their friends, family and political candidates. It is a week-long event for folks to show off the continued success of their family name and mounting wealth. Ownership of these cabins shows the privilege of this elite group, whose names give them the right to have a front row seat every year. But you can't drink—I mean, support political campaigns—by yourself. You invite extended family and friends, plus welcome the media, and of course politicians. And there you have it! The fun tradition of the Neshoba County Fair.

Politicians head back to their communities and neighborhoods for some final campaigning before Election Tuesday. They participate in the ritual of shaking hands, kissing babies, and, in the South, going to someone else's church on Sunday, to show you deserve their vote, too! You can tell when church members have heard that a certain candidate they really like is coming. At my church, you can smell the food, mid-sermon. The cooks are in the back listening to the sermon on the speakers as they prepare the feast for the pastor and his family, along with church officials and their families, the visiting candidate and his family, along with any other high profile politician who may not be up for re-election, but up for a good Sunday meal.

Tuesday is here. Every TV news producer who has an evening show, and the late newscast especially—that would be me, year after year—prays to their Heavenly Father a fervent prayer that promises to make their first born child become a pastor, minister, bishop, or priest, if He will just bless you to have a near-flawless election night newscast. Amen.

Well, I guess this night was not supposed to go like that for all involved. It turned out for some to be what our former sports director, and my friend, Mitchell Williams, taught me to be a "character building" night. Because what was to follow nearly blew my mind, and I have seen a lot of mind-blowing events in this business, and I am not easily stirred.

So the set-up was pretty simple and standard. We would have a reporter and photographer do a live shot at the state auditor's house. He was the incumbent and was probably going to win, despite attacks from his female opponent. That primary race became pretty heated and all eyes quickly turned to it. Stacey Pickering's opponent accused him of spending his campaign money on his daughter a car, and other stuff her camp thought worthy of putting in campaign ads. Pickering had spent the past year aggressively going after folks in office who were sticking their hand in the taxpayer's cookie jar. He sent a lot of them to do time and pay a fine.

He'd led in the polls all night, and we expected him to win. A couple of phone calls were made to his camp to make sure we could come to Pickering's house. They approved the live interview, and off to his house we go. The arrangements had to go through the proper channels, but I already knew we could come. I know Pickering's public relations manager, Jamel Major, and he told me it would get approved. He arranged a spread for our crew. Jamel and I used to work together. He was the best reporter I've ever seen. The boy was bad! Network material. He decided to go into public relations. That check is way better than a TV news reporter's check. Plus, most importantly, the hours are way better. Our crew was happy to go. TV people love covering stories where there is some good food and beverage, especially when it is free and in abundance. And Southern politicians love to show off. For some folks, presentation and perception is all that matters in politics. They'll hand you their vote on a silver platter. And don't have a legendary last name with a history in politics. Plus, have no scandal that can be proven or hasn't been in the headlines, and you are practically a shoo-in. So presentation and perception for a Southern politician is everything. It can not only get the candidate a vote this go round, but get them a repeat voter. Now, that voter can round up a new voter, who can round up even more shallow votes! A vote is a vote. A win's a win.

So our news crew showed up for what is not known yet to be an eventful night. Tony shows up first. Earlier in the day, he was acting crazy as if he didn't know where to go. I can't count the amount of times we have been to Pickering's house to get an interview with Tony being the photographer. So I have to give him directions to get there. My goodness! Google Maps! I really think there is a shortage upstairs for him. One day, I had to tell him again how to do the exact same thing he had done the day before and actually got right. He had the nerve to tell me he had been to sleep, and today was a new day. Huh? So your memory is wiped out by sleep? Lord! What kind of medication is he taking or, rather, abusing? Really? I am sure Tony makes Jesus question Tony's birth.

Graham arrives impeccably dressed. He is such a neat guy. He is very professional. He keeps to himself at work. Graham finds Tony and realizes he has set up in the wrong place. Tony was busy talking to Pickering's campaign manager. He likes to know everybody. I am sure you know folks like that.

"Hey, Tony," Graham says.

"Hey, Graham," Tony replies.

Graham then introduces himself to C. Jermaine Brown. He is Pickering's campaign manager. We grew up together. He is a twin. His brother and I are cool, too. C. Jerome Brown is in the banking industry. He holds a nice position at one of the local banks. Our parents went to college together and remained friends, so as kids, the Brown boys and I were always at each other's birthday parties, and social events, and we went to school together. We have remained friends.

Jermaine tells Graham, "Nice to meet you."

Before Jermaine could mention they were set up in the wrong place, Graham mentioned it. He and Jermaine had talked earlier over the phone. Jermaine told Graham they would need to set up on the patio that had such a beautiful manicured backyard behind it. I see why Pickering wanted to be back there. It was absolutely gorgeous! So Tony, who deems simple change as an act of congress, loses it, in front of the candidate's campaign manager, mind you, when Graham tells him they are not doing the live shot from inside the house, but outside.

"Well, Terrica said to go to the house and set up!" Tony says with tension in his voice. Terrica Washington's official title is assignment manager, but she's my bestie for life! We've been friends since college and have been through so much at this TV station. She tells the news reporters where to go, and who to meet up with if they are not shooting their own story and can't shoot a live shot by themselves. I'm sure at this point Graham wished he could set up by himself.

"Well, Tony, I am telling you I was told by his camp that we are setting up out back," Graham calmly spoke.

So Tony's spastic self, spazzes out and says loudly, "This is where I was told to set up, so this is where I set up! I am not sure why you got the wrong information."

"Wrong information, Tony?" Graham yelled. "I have the correct information given to me by Pickering's camp, who is standing right here in front of both of us!" Graham pointed out. "This is what I was told by his campaign manager, who you are looking at, fool. You need to get your shit together and move to the back patio like we were told; we do not have a lot of time as you can see before the show starts. Quit causing a scene," Graham added.

"Well, all I am saying is Terrica told me the house," Tony said, trying to get the last word in.

"Tony! Quit acting so damn crazy and move the fucking equipment to the back of the house! "NOW!" Graham replied.

At this point, a few people in the distance, not really hearing exactly what is going on, kind of turned around because they heard some elevated voices.

"Well, I will move. I just set up where I was told. That is all I am saying," Tony finished.

"Damn," Graham yelled, getting the last word in. Jermaine stood there the whole time, really not sure if he should step in or not. It all happened so fast. He just let it go on. Without a minute to spare, the live shot went off without a hitch! My show had very few mistakes. A couple of graphics were taken too slow and one super had a misspelled word. No technical errors. I will take it! Looks like my firstborn is going into the ministry!

I made it back to my desk and my desk phone rang. It is Tony.

"Uh, hey, Tam," he said.

"Hey, Tony," I replied.

I'm imagining what is about to come out of his mouth. You never know. He gives me his version of what happened at the live shot. He is innocent now. He was just doing what he was told, but Graham had other information, and he had to pack up his stuff and move.

I was like, "Okay, Tony, what was the big deal about moving?"

"Well, I guess it was not a big deal," he said. "I think Graham got a little upset with me because I think he thought I made him look like he didn't know what was going on in front of Pickering's campaign manager."

"Alright, Tony. Just come on back to the TV station," I said.

I hung up the phone. Just as I do that, I get a text from Jermaine that said, "Hey."

I text him back, "Hi, there! What are you going to tell me about my people? Lol!"

He replied, "Graham snapped on Tony!"

I text him back and explained that Tony had already told me and that Tony likes to be the first one to tell the story, by the way. I tell Jermaine it should not have happened. I apologized for the unprofessionalism. I went on to say that Tony is one-directional, and any change throws his being into outer space! He was told to set up at the house, and because he was not told specifically to set up on the back patio, it all became overwhelming for him. Normal people would just say okay and move. I did reiterate to Jermaine that Graham should not have snapped on Tony in front of him, but Tony is a lot to handle.

Jermaine texted back, "Ok…all good!"

I thanked him for the spread they laid out for the crew and congratulated him on Pickering's unofficial win. He got the most votes that night, despite the negative ad campaigns. I guess people favor the guy who isn't scared to go after the elected officials who misuse taxpayer's money. Plus, the nice backdrop did not hurt, I am sure.

Graham made it back to the station before Tony. He told me what happened. I told him what Tony said. He admitted he should not have lost his cool. I told him to make sure he called Jermaine the next day to apologize. He said he would. I warned him that others there may have heard what was going on and may call management, and be prepared to answer to that. He said okay. Poor kid looked wiped out. Here comes Tony, all high energy, to bring back the equipment. It amazes me the person that causes the most ruckus acts like nothing is wrong!

I made it through the primaries. Lord, please help me through the general election in November. More prayers and more of my babies going into the ministry!

8.
When the headline story comes to the TV station, literally

I WAS ON my way to a spring-and-summer shopping spree with my mom one weekend. I love clothes, shoes, watches, purses, jewelry, make-up, pedis, manis, and everything else in-between.

My mom, out of the blue, said to me, "You have never once said you hate your job."

I told her that's because I really like what I do. Being a TV news producer is quite enjoyable and entertaining. Now, I will say that I haven't always been crazy about the rude viewers that called in, nor some of the people/personalities I've had to work with, but those were few.

So I thought one day. One thing about working in the news business is that you experience a lot of aggravation with crazy people, calling the station with every problem under the sun they know you have the answer to, but you don't. Nobody does.

I had a lady call in one time about lights she saw in the sky, and the passenger with her, who obviously saw these same lights, wanted to know what they were. Huh? This crazy conversation continued with me trying to figure out what in the hell they were talking about. They each took turns going back and forth on the car's speakerphone system to plead their case. Note, they could work a car's hands-free system, but couldn't figure out what the lights were in the sky. They even went as far to say, reluctantly, I may add, they thought it was some type of UFO. What? Was this shit for real? I didn't have time for this. Then it hit me after they described the light in the sky that it was strobe lights they were seeing. The kind people use at night at a club, or some big event they're having. You know, the ones that shine circles that cross back and forth, chasing one another in a circular pattern. I remembered the convention center had some huge event going on. We did a live shot preview of the event in the 5 p.m. newscast. Lord, have mercy please. Once I described to a tee exactly what they were seeing, they were satisfied and said, "Sorry to have bothered you, but we just didn't know what was going on." Did they think they were about to get beamed up? Help us, Lord!

    That would not be the last time I would hear from a viewer. Come on. Do not interrupt regular scheduled programming at a TV station. Even during a natural disaster! So, the days after Hurricane Katrina were horrible. Working sixteen-hour days with no power, nor running water. Weeks before, Florida was getting hit back-to-back with hurricanes. I looked at that as I had to make sure I ran the latest storm update in my newscast. Now, I was the story. We were so tired. We were broadcasting interstate, highway, street closings, and other information to viewers who couldn't even see us. Most places, other than medical facilities that got power first, were without power for eleven days. Trust me. That is forever when it happens to you. Plus, we had to work in the same conditions as folks in homes that were destroyed, or heavily damaged. Guess that wasn't much better, either. Day in and day out, we were without cash, gas, and hot food, and having to sit in long lines to get ice, water and whatever else someone had compassion to give out. One of our local sheriffs, Sheriff Billy McGee, was accused of commandeering a supply truck carrying ice and other stuff. It was headed to a central location, where its contents could have been left for days, to be distributed later. I swear, the red tape of government. He wasn't having it. He helped a lot of people survive that day by giving out everything that was on it! He may have even given away the truck's steering wheel if somebody needed it. He was a hero. I think they later wanted to arrest him. Crazy. Katrina was absolutely the worst thing I've ever experienced. Everybody, no matter how much money they made or already had, was knocked down to the same level: in a line wanting some help. The streets and interstates were blocked with debris. It was hard for anyone to get around, and when you finally got out, you were scared you were going to run out of gas, so neighbors were carpooling to go wait hours in line, just to get the very basics.

Things started to get back to normal in the coming weeks. Power was back on to every community, except for some rural areas that were last on the list. People could get our broadcasts now and were glued to the TV around the clock, waiting for us to give information about who had power, who didn't, and when those that didn't were going to get it. They were also glued to the screen to find out when schools, some of which had been heavily damaged, were going to reopen, and what businesses were starting to open back up for folks to get food, household items, and lumber to build back their homes. Plus, they were tuning in to find out when they had to get back to work.

Well, of course, people were at home with nothing to do, and I'm sure their kids really had nothing to do, so that probably drove some households toward borderline child abuse. And then there was NASCAR! Yes! Sports will always bring people together. Something to rally around! After weeks of suffering and property loss, the joy of NASCAR being interrupted, even to bring important information to homes after a natural disaster, appeared not to be welcome. The phones in the newsroom rang out, one telephone line after another, to a point where the sound is nonstop. This goes on for several minutes. Folks in the newsroom, including me, are about to lose our minds. The reason for this outburst was that we continued to broadcast after the NASCAR race started. Ontario, one of our reporters, received an important roadway opening from the Transportation Department that we felt we had to get on. They asked us to please get the new information on immediately. Now, we had broadcast all the newest information we had, so we started back up with the race, and the phones finally stopped ringing. Thank you, Lord! Well, that was short lived.

The big blow up came when we interrupted NASCAR again to broadcast that someone really in need called in about needing supplies for a newborn baby. They had been stuck at their home all this time and ran out of supplies and couldn't get out to get them. Their car had a tree still on it. So we decided to broadcast it and, in return, a viewer called us wanting to deliver baby supplies.

Some viewers didn't seem to care about the needs of those people, and we started snatching up the phones once again to answer them. The calls continued back-to-back.

Quin, the producer in the booth this go-around, tells our news director-slash-main anchor about all the nasty attitudes of the viewers calling in, asking if we really have to keep cutting away from NASCAR. In case you noticed, we have to be the only station left where the news director also anchors. He loves the limelight most of all and wants the check of a news director. It must be nice to be the longtime buddy of the general manager who lets him have both titles, plus a massive salary. Well, by now he's been on the desk for quite some time with no break. Why, I don't know. There are plenty of anchors available to take over. Again, he enjoys being the face of the TV station. Well, this last notice about the phones still ringing off the hook sent him over the edge.

He flipped out on live TV. It got real folks! He got fed up with NASCAR fans calling in and complaining. The incident went something like this. I can't quote it exactly, but this is what I remember: "Some of you people need to get your priorities straight. People are suffering, and we are trying to get this information out to them. We have some NASCAR fans out there calling in constantly about wanting to see this race, but this is a matter of life and death for some folks, and it bugs the HELL out of me that some of you don't realize this. GET OFF OUR DAMN PHONES!"

I think there was more, something along the lines of "and another thing." I don't really remember the rest of what he said. I just know we all heard it, and it brought a smile to our faces, and the phones literally stopped ringing. Ain't nothing like a good cursing out sometimes to put you in check. I mean, is watching a TV program that serious?

And, please, do not interrupt programming for an elderly

military veteran. They are close to my heart. My grandfather, Joseph Alvin Jackson served in World War II. This one night we got a call from someone who we found out later on was a Vietnam War veteran.

He called in and Rusty answered the phone. I heard Rusty scrambling trying to answer the caller's questions. Finally, he put the man on speakerphone. Lord!

All I hear is, "I fucking hate y'all. I don't give a damn about what is on, I want to see Wheel of Fortune."

Prior to Rusty putting him on speaker, I had whispered to Rusty to tell him that we were airing a D-Day special, thinking this would appease him, shut him down, and force him to apologize for cursing us out. Nope!

The next thing out of his mouth was, "I don't give a shit about fucking D-Day! I am a Vietnam Vet. And another thing! It's too much nomenclature on the screen."

A few storms were popping up in the forecast, so master control popped up the radar map with the counties that had watches and warnings in our viewing area. It's a small transparent map of counties to the bottom left of the screen, plus we were scrolling across the top of the screen the affected counties. Well, Rachel was listening in on this call as well. She was drawn in like the rest of us, and was shocked, and couldn't believe what was coming out of his mouth. By this time, the sports guys and camera ops were listening in, too! We were all kind of laughing because it seemed so unreal for someone to call a TV station and act like this because they couldn't watch a particular TV show. So Rachel asked him what nomenclature meant in between our giggles. Hell, I didn't know what it meant either. He was happy to explain and educate us, and share his disgust about the fact that it was too much going on, in his opinion, across his TV screen. He decided he was tired of us and hung up. We talked about that call for weeks!

At least he didn't come out to the TV station. Well, I spoke too soon because one day somebody did. So what else can get you talking for weeks at a time? When someone physically shows up at the TV station to show you God in his car. Yep! This happened. There's never been security at the station. We have been so blessed that nothing major has ever happened to us. We've gotten threats several times, including one time in the mid to late 90's, when I first started working at the station. Can you believe I had never experienced racism up until this point? It was during the trials of some old KKK members for the murder of civil rights leader, Vernon Dahmer, Sr. many years ago. Mr. Dahmer helped register Black people to vote back in the 60's. Never take your right to vote for granted. Our state legislature finally recognized him for his efforts. January 10th is Vernon Dahmer Day! Good for his family. They are such nice people. I'm glad to know them.

Broadcast, Bloopers & Boneheads

The building has never been secure, except for our keycard system that was installed just days after I started working at the station. An employee came back to the station after being fired and threatened to harm the sales manager. Keycard system installed.

But this particular day started out crazy before I even got to the station with an email from Diana, a member of the web team. She's pretty intense in breaking news situations, or a work crisis, or sometimes, just a regular ol'day! Kathryn, a new member of the web team, just tries to keep up. She has managed to fit into the circus and do a good job. I didn't quite know how to take Diana's email that said "there is a person in the parking lot that we are concerned about." The email went on to say "he is on the phone with our news director and is acting strangely. The sheriff's department was on the way. If you are in the building, please do not leave the building." As I read this, I figured by the time I got to the station this would all be over. Sure enough, a few minutes later, Diana sent another email that said the man had left the parking lot.

I got to work and asked what the heck had been going on. Everyone chimed in with their version of what had happened. You know news people like to tell their story. One by one, they shared their take on it. It was a funny story to tell since all was well. One person told me how all the engineers, Mr. Clyde, Ricky

D, Paxton, and Mr. Rick all went out into the parking lot to talk to him. He talked about God sitting in the passenger seat of his vehicle. Another person mentioned how the guy wanted us to do a story on how we need peace in the world. Someone else mentioned how he talked about how his parents had done him wrong. Then, I listened to someone tell me how the engineers were about to get physical with the man once they saw him pick up some rocks from the flower garden, near the door to the receptionist lobby area. They quickly started screaming at him. He kept on going as if he was in his own little world. He was mumbling something that no one could understand. His body language remained calm. No sudden moves or anything. He just went about what he was doing as if no one else was around him. Well, just as the group was about to have enough of this guy, guess what he did with the rocks? He stacked them in some kind of Zen pattern! What? Everyone there really didn't know what to do at this point. The guy didn't seem aggressive, but certainly, something was wrong with him. He's out at a TV station in the middle of the day; well, he and God are there, for no other reason than to ramble on. So by this time, Mr. Rick had enough. He was tired of this guy not listening, nor leaving. He lifted up his shirt, so the man could see his weapon that he had retrieved from his truck while the others had distracted our new friend. Now, we are not supposed to have particular weapons on station property, but

I heard HR didn't even care in the heat of the moment. Mrs. Beth probably checked her vehicle hoping she had one! I heard she had her husband's hunting truck. She needed some work done to her car and took his hunting truck. Yep, we are in the South, baby! Men have hunting trucks in addition to their regular vehicle, and it is usually tricked out. They said HR was so glad somebody could defend us, in case shit got real, because the sheriff's deputies didn't make it before the guy left! Of course, they showed up afterward! I guess Mr. Rick, who is ex-military and who I imagine in my head is a former spy in the Air Force during the 80's, must have made an impression on this loco, and he decided to leave. Mr. Rick looks to still be as tough as he was back then! I'm behind Mr. Rick if and when it goes down!

We had been back to work, and back to normal, for an hour or so after each person had told their part of the story. Other than the crazy man in the parking lot, it had been a regular news day, until Mr. Rick burst into the newsroom from the door to the parking lot to tell me the man had returned. What? We thought we had gotten rid of him. I ran to our general manager's office, where our news director was, to tell them that the man was back, and we needed to call the sheriff again, in hopes this time they'd show up! Diana immediately stopped updating the web and sent out another email that said, "don't leave the building. The man had returned and is in the parking lot." At this point, I wanted to see what this joker looked like. So I went outside and, to my surprise, he looked super young. I said this out loud, and Sommer, who was standing behind me and looking on as well, said that they were told the boy said he's twenty-two. The engineers had him cornered as if to say he wouldn't get away this time. I'd had enough. I went back inside. I just wanted to see what he looked like. Rusty came in a little bit after me and told us the sheriff's deputies made it this time and arrested the guy. Rusty texted me a picture of the guy handcuffed. Plus, this fool had weed in the passenger's seat of his truck. Authorities found it once they searched the truck, before the tow truck guy towed it away. Lord, what a day! I guess God, the person in the young man's passenger seat, couldn't speak to the cops on this joker's behalf to say He was holding the weed for him!

9.
If you don't tell anybody your business, won't anybody know your business!

NOW, I'M TRYING to stack a show, and I'm in need of a live shot at 6 p.m. So before I can decide what story I am going live with, Felicia called my desk phone to tell me she wanted to go live with her story. Well, I forgot last week it was mentioned that management didn't want to go live with Felicia on her last week at the station. Apparently, they are nervous about her doing something crazy live on air. Why they are worried about this, I don't know. Felicia has never seemed like the type of chick to do that. Maybe they are paranoid from that Alaska reporter, mad about some marijuana ordinance, who said, "Fuck it, I quit!" live on air that time. I know the whole crew on that news set spazzed out. That was great TV! Can you imagine watching that happen from home? I watched it on the Internet, with the curse word bleeped out, and that was entertaining enough. I'm sure this was a nightmare for management and the owners of the station. Oh, well, that's why they get paid the big bucks. Handle it!

Anywho, Felicia explained to me what her story was about.

"Hey, Tam, a local restaurant is having a cocktail hour fundraiser to help the zoo buy two flamingos."

"Awwh, That's a great idea," I replied.

She goes on to explain the cocktail is called the Pink Flamingo, and all proceeds will be given to the zoo. Many other businesses are doing well by the zoo because, last week, a bunch of frat boys at the university decided to do a little hazing. The guys being hazed were only supposed to break into the zoo and take a selfie with the flamingos. Well, one overachiever pledge in the group decided to steal one. I've learned flamingos are very delicate creatures. Her leg broke, and the frat boys tossed her out. Yep! Tossed her out on the side of the road. Police and zoo workers found her alive, but had to euthanize her. Wow! How awful, right? Well, the story gets worse. Her male companion back at the zoo isolated himself from the rest of the stand. Zookeepers said he was sad and depressed. He died a few days later. They said he was lonely without her. I guess he couldn't go on without the love of that good woman! Only in the animal world! How many times has Larry King married? Ha!

So I thought. I had to beat around the bush with Felicia as to why we will not do the live shot from there. Then, I realized. There really was a reason why we couldn't do it. I guess the others haven't heard.

"We are having problems with the Live U's, Felicia," I said.

"What's wrong with them?" she asked.

"I was told Coleman had to do a software upgrade on them and, as usual, when we do an upgrade to anything around here, in my experience, it never goes right the first time," I explained.

"Oh, ok. I remember something like that happening before," she said.

"Yeah, I don't know why the rest of them haven't heard," I said. She was finally satisfied with my reason and went back to her desk.

Now, the news director comes to my desk and gives me the low-down. Apparently, he, and everybody else in the newsroom, knows about Felicia and the married chef. What? Lord! How do they know? Now, she told me about him some weeks ago. How she was having a lovely time with him, and how he would call her over for dinner and cook whatever she wanted. I would love to date a chef, but not a married one. She told me he's in the process of a divorce, and they don't live together anymore. A man will tell you anything, but she's convinced they no longer love each other as husband and wife. I didn't ask, but I hoped she didn't tell anyone else in the newsroom about this. Plus, he is older than her, too. She's close to Willow, the web girl, who I don't trust and feel would be her Linda Tripp if you know what I mean. The kind that doesn't want anyone in her business but will tell your business to every ear that will listen.

Anyways, the news director goes on to say he and the guy are friends, well, friends through some fantasy football league. Uh oh! And that he owns the restaurant that is having the fundraiser tonight. Wow, I didn't know that! He won't disclose how he thinks he knows the guy and Felicia have been hooking up, but we all know men talk more than women! They tell everybody, even when it's not true, whereas we tell our best friend. So I'm thinking the married chef told him he is hooking up with one of his reporters, which probably isn't true. Men lie all the time about who they are hooking up with.

So I go, "Yeah, she told me she was seeing someone that is a chef and he is in the process of getting a divorce."

So he goes, "Oh, I'm right?" as if he doesn't completely know if it's true or not.

Like the chef didn't say something to him. Yeah, right! Who is he to judge? He is divorced. I heard his ex-wife is near flawless. You figure out what happened. I'm sure he is not the one to talk about who's hooking up with someone.

He goes on to tell me he is not covering a story to give free advertisement to someone because she is sleeping with him. He said Felicia did a story last week about a woman who cooks and sells food out of her food truck, and is now opening up a restaurant. Well, the chef, A.K.A. married guy, is the one financing it all! I didn't know this! So he puts two and two together, I guess, and decide we are not doing another story where he is involved.

So, now, Felicia has had time to think and comes back to my desk. She said she knows why we are not doing the live shot.

"Tam, I know the real reason why we are not doing the live shot," she said with an attitude.

"Why?" I asked.

"It's because of his brother," she replied.

I forgot for a second that his brother owns that new restaurant in town.

"He doesn't want another restaurant getting airtime and business from folks seeing the story on TV, she said."

If she only knew what he was thinking.

"I can't believe this, it's for a really good cause," she said walking back to her desk.

I still think Felicia told Willow's fake-friend ass, about the chef, and then, Willow told the masses not to tell it. You know how that goes. Don't tell anybody your business, and won't anybody know your business.

At this point, breaking news turns all of our attention elsewhere. Terrica got a phone call from one of her sources that the city council president's daughter got arrested for a D.U.I. last night. Uh-oh now! The source told her to check the jail docket. So we did and couldn't find her name on it anywhere. That's odd. It's as if she was never arrested. Now, we are all curious because Terrica's source is a very reliable one. So what really happened? We couldn't find anything official on it to report. So we went to the street committee to find out what is really going on. And the streets are talking. We didn't have to go far. Several of our interns were at the party—I mean fundraiser. Since we know of the situation now, they spilled the beans. Apparently, the council president's daughter attended a fraternity fundraiser, plus the after party, and had a little too much underage drinking and decided to drive herself home. The sophomore was almost home but didn't quite keep in her lane, so she got pulled over by a cop. Between the time she got pulled over and made it to jail, she must have contacted the city council president, her daddy. He either is there before she arrives, or in time enough to take care of things before she is booked in. Either way, she made it home with no record of her criminal behavior. And we had no way of proving it happened last night. Terrica called her source back and told him we can't find any record of it happening. He told her to request the dash-cam video of the arresting officer and gave us his name. Oh, we've got something now. We thought.

Someone thought to fill out the F.O.I.A, Freedom of Information Act form, to request the officer's dash-cam video. We got stopped, dead in our tracks by our news director. Yep! See, the council and the mayor have been at odds for several months now. Well, three of the five council members, including the council president, which obviously is the majority. And we have been at every council meeting with cameras rolling to catch the circus for the viewers. How do we know when the circus is coming to town? The council president has our news director on speed dial. That's how! We know the city's business before the mayor does! I thought council members, including the council president and the mayor, are supposed to work together, but, in this case, it seems the council president is happy to throw the mayor under the bus by letting our news director know about things most council presidents don't tell the news director at the local TV station. Most city governments don't want the media in their city business. Well, for that matter, nobody wants the media in their business.

Our news director is happy to oblige because he's been against the mayor since day one. It's not for reasons you think. Usually, when someone puts stumbling blocks in place for someone else, it's because they have done something to them. Well, that's not the case here. It's guilt by association. See, the mayor's best friend is a pastor in the area. The pastor and news director have been feuding since I can remember. Do you want to know why? They are two peas in a pod. They each want to be in control of everything coming and going. They want to hobnob with people they consider to be in the upper echelon of life. They both like to be recognized and want to be seen on TV all the time. Our news director enjoys anchoring, and the pastor's Sunday service airs on our station. Needless to say, they are both recognized in our community. Okay, so what really started the feud? I can't remember exactly, but I can tell you about an incident I remember during the feud.

Let me set up some background for you. Several employees, who work behind the scenes and on-air, go to the pastor's church. Now, combine that with a news director who will say what he feels on set about people, including the pastor, before the show and during commercial breaks, when his mic remains hot. He talks low to his co-anchor sometimes, but we just cue his mic in the control room to hear what he is saying. A couple of those in-studio camera operators don't have to hear it through a mic, they are right there to listen hard to every word. Did I mention one camera operator is the pastor's deacon's son and the other camera operator is his nephew? So you can imagine what gets back to the pastor. Well, the pastor says what he feels about people, too, and somehow, someway, what he said this particular day got back to his archrival. Game on!

So, the news director was all riled up as he made it to the news set. And, like clockwork, he said something during the commercial break.

"Certain religious leaders in the area should watch what they say," he said, trying to talk low.

His co-anchor whispers, "What are you talking about?"

"I was told of something that was overheard, that Rev. Lowdown said," he told her.

"You think it's about us running that story last week?" she asked.

"Probably so," he responded.

One of the news director's buddies was having lunch where the reverend frequently has lunch. Their booths were back-to-back, and the guy overheard what the reverend thought he was saying privately to his lunch date. It was somewhat threatening. Something along the lines of if he could see him face-to-face, referring to our news director, he would knock him out! The man told his buddy, the news director, just that. Now, why would Rev. Lowdown want to knock out the news director? Well, last week we did a story about the reverend's son getting pulled over for speeding. He was doing over 70 miles an hour and was found to have been high from something. We see these arrests on the jail docket all the time. But when it's Rev. Lowdown's son, the news director has to run it, so we did.

After my 6 o'clock show was over, we all headed back to the newsroom. I go to my desk, like everyone else does. Sometime later, the news director locked his door and started to leave.

He stopped by my desk and said, "I'm headed down to city hall to see what's going down there."

I said, "Okay, see you later," as I went back to what I was doing on my computer.

It crossed my mind *why is he going down there?* But I kept on doing what I was doing. We did the live shot from the city council meeting that they had earlier as they usually do every other Tuesday, but the meeting was over. A few people may still be there, but what was his business with them? Anywho, I didn't think anything else about it until the next day, when I got a phone call.

My phone rings.

"Hello?" I said.

"Hey, Tam," he said.

"Hey, DW! What's going on with you? I replied.

DW is the assistant to the mayor and has been for almost a year and a half. DW is my good friend. I've known him since college. I was the freshman coming in late to my 8 o'clock class every morning. He points that out still to this day. I've never been a morning person. He was a senior who played football and was always on time because he had been up since 5:30 for practice. Southern Miss to the Top! He also used to be one of our reporters, *In the City with Devin Whitley.* Our news director would talk about Devin behind his back; well, hell, he talked about all of us like that. Then he would bend over backwards to help us out in a jam. He is a very complex individual. When his marriage was on the rocks, he ran to DW to pray for him. DW is also an ordained minister. See, this business can lead you down the road of righteousness if you choose it. Then again, this same business will eat you alive and have you making back-door deals and sinning all over the place if you choose that. Life really is about choices.

I was not prepared for what he was about to share with me.

"Not too much, girl, how are you doing?" he said.

"I'm well, thanks." I replied.

"I saw your boss last night," he started to tell me.

"You did? Where? I asked.

"At city hall," he said.

"City hall? He mentioned going down there last night when he was leaving here. What was he down there for?" I asked.

"To get into a fight," he replied.

"A fight? What do you mean, a fight? With whom?" I questioned.

"With the reverend," he responded.

"What?" I yelled.

"The reverend? You have got to be kidding me! Who saw it? I haven't heard anything about this!" I said, with so much excitement in my voice.

"And you won't hear nothing about it," he said.

"WHAT HAPPENED JOKER? Tell it!" I said.

DW started to tell me how it all went down! The city council meeting had ended. The mayor, DW, the reverend, Councilwoman Delgado, a bank manager, and a handful of other folks had stayed back to talk about some upcoming project. Here comes my fearless news director. He mingled with some of the folks he knew there. The reverend saw him. He saw the reverend. The reverend walked over to another group of people that were talking. My news director joined them. DW said he didn't notice what was going on until he heard loud voices arguing. He turned around and saw his old boss lunge and swing at the good reverend. He barely missed him, but, luckily, he did because I know the reverend would have pressed charges. It would have made front page news all over the local media outlets, their websites and social media. DW said he jumped in and grabbed his former boss since he was the closest to him. Somebody else grabbed the reverend. I am in tears laughing by this point.

"DW? What did the reverend say to him for him to throw a punch at him?" I said.

"Apparently, your boss came in telling the reverend to say what he needed to say to his face and not send messages. The reverend said he had no problem telling him to his face just how he felt about him. They went back and forth. Then, the reverend told him he was a coward, just like his daddy! And that's when I turned around and saw your boss try to land a punch." DW finished.

"Dang! What happened to 'don't talk about my momma because we'll have to fight if you talk about my momma'? I guess that goes for daddies too now," I said, barely able to be heard over my laughter.

So you can imagine over the years how bad this feud has continued. Every chance my news director got to throw the good ol' reverend and anybody, and I mean anybody, associated with him under the bus, he did.

People in the community noticed, especially folks in other city governments in our coverage area. They were in awe, but at the same time, content because that meant we didn't come snooping around their city government for a story. We didn't even go to their council meetings to just find out what was on their agendas. Someone could have been stealing all that city's money, and we would never uncover it because of the focus on just one city's politics because of one news director's grudge with a pastor.

Even now that the old news director is gone, it continues. Bad blood between our TV station, even with new management, and city hall remains. They don't even understand that they are pawns, carrying out a feud created by two men that are not even relevant anymore. They have the nerve to think that I care enough to go tell the mayor. I do not care! Our families know each other very well. I don't even have the mayor's personal cell number, though, but I could have it in the time it would take me to text him on his work number to get it! Just like that. I'm too smart to be a pawn and to get caught up in something that nobody can explain. It's too many layers to unravel to even figure out what started it all. But each year, new eager beaver reporters get sucked into the feud. It's like watching the Hatfields and the McCoys. Again, I don't have time to care. I have a book to write. And they keep supplying me with material! Another day at the TV news circus!

10.
Why do co-worker's relationships become part of my day?

IT WAS THE summer of interns. I was surprised there were so many at the TV station during the summer semester. Most of them usually go home. I thought, *maybe these guys graduate at the end of summer and got to get that last minute internship in.* We usually get the dozens of interns during the fall and spring semesters. I remember my senior year and having to gather my thoughts about what I had left to take to finally get out of college. I was ready to go!

Thank God, I didn't have to deal with all the eager beavers and having to listen to their enthusiasm about the business. That job goes to Miranda Beard, our lovely assistant news director. Little do these kids know, I guess, about how fast those six months are going to pass by, and those student loan payments kick in on that salary for a new job in a small TV news market. Lord, do I remember. If I could go back to my freshman year knowing what I know now, I would have skipped out on this major, I do believe.

I got to work and no interns around my desk! Yes! They had been given their assignments already. I checked out the web and social media in peace.

Well, that was short-lived! There came Brooklyn Ward, one of the newest interns in the news department, headed toward my desk. She looked a little frazzled. I didn't want her to share why because then I would be involved. Please, don't share! Ugh! She began to share.

She began to explain how she met Sarah. Sarah is Samson's wife. Sam is the evening weatherman. Now, each time Sarah and Sam had a baby, Sam would bring the baby to work at night, and I would babysit them in the control room. It was a running joke how I was the night nanny. I didn't mind. He would feed and change them, and so by the time the show started, he would bring them in their carrier to the control room and sit them by my chair, and they would just fall asleep. I guess Sarah would give him a hard time about his night schedule and not being around to bond with them and not to mention she needed a break.

Not only was Brooklyn interested in news, but weather also, so she's kind of leaning more toward an internship in weather and had started to like it. This particular day, she was really excited! The weather department had gotten a new weather graphics package with the latest bells and whistles. Sam had come in early that day to learn about the new system from the guy sent to install it. So by the time Brooklyn made it to the weather center, Sam was so ready to show someone what this system could do. So he was excited to see the wide-eyed weather intern. She sat down, and Sam showed her how to use the system. After about forty-five minutes or so, Sam excused himself. Brooklyn decided to try to build her own weathercast. She was so excited to get some hands on experience outside of the classroom, and she was actually doing a good job. Just as she goes to build her seven-day graphic, she hears someone making a lot of noise coming around the corner. It's a woman's voice and sounds like she's on her cell phone and has plastic bags in her hands. Sure enough, in walks a lady getting off her cell phone with several shopping bags in her hand that she's never seen before. It's Sarah.

Oooooweee! Now, I love me some Sarah, but she is just straight up. She doesn't fool with everyone. Some of the ladies up here she's known since she was a child, and they are in her mom's social circle, and she knows their dirt, including past affairs, current affairs, husbands, and ex-husbands. She also knows the fathers of the children these ladies say are their husband's children. She'll walk right past some of them and not speak. It tickles me so and gets me to wondering about their skeletons. Southerners know culturally how important it is to speak to people you pass by, even if you don't like them but especially your husband's co-workers. The ladies talk about her when she leaves.

They know to wait until she is out of the building. She ain't fake. With Sarah, what comes up comes out. She won't hesitate to confront any of them about what she's heard they've said about her. She's confronted one of them here before. Folks talked about it for weeks. She's not the typical wannabe demure southern belle who waits two seconds after you have left to talk about you. I love that about her. She's really down to earth, and she loves me to death. She makes a beeline straight to my desk when she comes to the newsroom, barely acknowledging anyone else, except for some of the ones that have been at the station for years. Now, she comes from *old money*. In the South, that means it's so much money you can barely count it all, and it has earned so much interest and has been passed down through the generations. Trust me, they are living on the interest. I heard her grandmother is sitting on so much money, it ain't even funny! And I'm told she has it all willed to Sarah and her mother, who is the grandmother's daughter. But looking at Sarah, you can't tell. She keeps it so basic. Except for an expensive piece here and there. Probably birthday or Christmas presents. Plus, I think her grandmother makes her earn her own money because she knows Sarah would kill herself if she controlled that much money.

Sarah looks disheveled and hot and sweaty, with several department store bags in her hands. Brooklyn quickly remembers its like ninety-four degrees outside today. Sarah introduced herself.

"I'm Sarah, Sam's wife, and you are?"

Brooklyn smiled and answered, "I'm Brooklyn, the intern, nice to meet you!"

Focused on how pretty Brooklyn is, Sarah asked, "How long have you been interning with Sam?"

"Just a couple of weeks for this summer semester," Brooklyn said.

Sarah then asked, "Where is Sam?"

"He stepped out for a second." Brooklyn said. "Would you like to have a seat and wait on him?"

Sarah had a look on her face, like, *who is this girl offering me a seat in my man's office?* Sarah sits down in Sam's chair, as if to claim her spot on the throne as queen. She unloads all of those shopping bags that Brooklyn thought odd for her to have brought with her to her husband's job. Brooklyn sees how uncomfortable Sarah's body language is coming across and attempts to compliment her. She notices Sarah has a handbag.

"Wow, I love your Louis Vuitton bag. My mom has the exact same one!"

All Sarah hears is "mom" and thinks Brooklyn must see her as a mom and not as her competition. Really? Competition? Sam is all right. He ain't no hot twenty-something-year-old like Brooklyn. He may have been, but he ain't today. Sarah is really putting him on a pedestal. Nobody wants Sam but Sarah, and nobody wants Sarah but Sam. And besides, Brooklyn is twenty-one years old, and Sam is pushing forty. So is Sarah. Plus, Sam brings home a small market TV non-management salary. Meaning, he can't be nobody's sugar daddy and barely has enough money to support Sarah and the kids, while she's all up in there with all those shopping bags. Probably used her mom's credit card. Her mom is quite a classy lady, a professor at the local university. She is a true southern belle. Well, except for being divorced and fine with it after twenty-five years of marriage. Sarah's dad was a hardworking, self-made, man who fell in love with Sarah's mom. He didn't have to have all the social connections and just grew apart from his wife's interests. Guess Sarah is a little like her daddy.

Sarah, candidly, said, "My mom got this bag for me after I didn't speak to her, or bring the kids around, for about a month."

Too much information! Brooklyn thought. Sarah turned around and complimented Brooklyn on her dress.

"That's a pretty dress you have on."

Brooklyn thought so, too! The dress cost a pretty penny. Her boyfriend's cheating ass had to drop some major coins on that Gucci dress.

With a big pretty smile, Brooklyn said, "Thank you!"

Sarah replied, without looking up as she dug through her

Louis bag, "It's a little short though to come to an internship at a news station, don't you think?

Before she gave Brooklyn a chance to respond, she said, "Kinda looks like a club dress to me."

At a loss for words, Brooklyn said, "Well, it's not a club dress."

Just in the nick of time, Sam walked into the weather office, to Brooklyn's relief and, to his surprise, to see Sarah.

"Hey baby!" Sam said, with a higher-than-normal pitch in his voice. "Have you met Brooklyn? She's the weather intern."

"Yes, we've met," said Sarah. "We were just talking about fashion."

Sam steps over all the bags he's wondering about.

"What are all these bags for, honey?"

"Well, a few things are for me, but these are clothes for the birthday party." Sarah said, with such excitement in her voice.

"But it's just one of our kids' birthday, these bags seem to have clothes for all of them." Sam said, as he looks briefly through the bags.

It really did look like clothes for three or four kids, Brooklyn thought. She had started to excuse herself from the room when Sam arrived, but it got interesting real quick, and her curiosity wouldn't let her leave. Plus, Sam had decided to look through the bags. He was blocking Brooklyn from getting up to say she was leaving.

"Well, yes, baby," Sarah said. "I got all the kids something to wear for the party. I didn't want the girls to not look as polished as the birthday boy, honey."

"Sarah," Sam said rather firmly as he lit a cigarette in the weather office that is, like the rest of the building, smoke free.

"I'm not understanding this right now. We just bought the girls new outfits for your best friend Kim's kid's birthday two weekends ago, Sarah," Sam said firmly again.

Sarah, a little heated about Sam's aggressive tone, plus she realizes the well put-together intern that reminds her of her friend Kim, is still in the room, said, "Well, dammit, Sam! They are not wearing what they wore to that party because those people will be at this party and think the kids don't have any more clothes!"

Sam said, really loud, "Well, sweetheart, I don't give a damn about what they think! We are fitting this party into our budget in the first place, and those new clothes are not in the budget. Maybe the birthday boy's clothes you can keep, but the girl's clothes have to go back."

Sarah stands up at this point, snatches the lit cigarette from between Sam's lips, throws it in the trash and says,

"Look here! Ain't nobody telling you not to buy cartons of cigarettes, nor that Johnnie Walker Black Label Deluxe Blend scotch whiskey you keep in that drawer over there," as she turned and pointed to his desk drawer.

Brooklyn's eyes got big, and her thoughts were *these two are off the chain!* She remembered looking at the company handbook and having a gun in a company car, or on company property, was against the rules, and she couldn't remember if she read in the handbook about having liquor at work in the desk drawer, but she had a feeling that's against the rules, too.

"Oh, you wanna go there, do you? Okay, okay!" Sam roared. "I found a bottle of pills with someone else's name on it, mixed in behind the Tony Chachere's in the spice cabinet at the house!"

I remembered someone saying the two met in rehab. I guess it's true! Sam had always been a professional as far as I could tell.

"Why are you in the spice cabinet anyways?" Sarah asked. "You won't even cook one night of the week to help me out! Weekends either!"

"Well, somebody has to work so you can have all these shopping bags to carry," Sam shouted.

Brooklyn decided she'd been entertained enough and should leave. She felt even if Sarah left right now, Sam would still be frazzled, and he wouldn't do a good job of showing her how to work the new weather software, anyways. And besides, she wanted to give him a chance to get himself together in time for the evening newscast. Plus, he may need a cigarette, and a shot of scotch that he hides in his drawer after all that he just went through. She wanted to give him some privacy since he had always been so nice to her after she asked if he could train her to do weather.

So, after sharing all of this with me, she told me she was about to leave. She was leaving earlier than usual today, anyway, and had okay'd it with Miranda. I told the poor child go on, and I would see her tomorrow.

Sam made it through all the evening shows like a champ. I'm sure Sarah will be back soon. I look forward to her bee lining it to my desk to speak to me.

11.
The life of TV news vehicles & equipment

I'VE BEEN BROUGHT up to always take care of what you have so that the Lord will show you favor and bless you with more. Why would God bless you with being able to afford that Mercedes when you won't even get regular oil changes for that Kia your parents bought you? Why would you lose parts to your work-issued camera, plus drop it when you treat your new iPhone like a newborn? I guess it's easy for some folks not to take care of something they didn't buy.

The other day, the sports guy, Austin, had to use the spare news camera. His camera had been having some issues and had to be taken to engineering. He was in a hurry to get to his shoot and couldn't wait for it to be fixed. He stopped by the spare equipment closet to pick up the spare camera to use. He loaded it up and left for his shoot. Everything really should have been in it, right? It's not used on a regular basis to have much damage, or any missing parts. Poor kid gets to his shoot and is missing so many parts he can't even do his job. Luckily, the coach was running behind for the interview. That gave him enough time to call Jonathan, the other sports guy, back at the station, to run him what he needed. It's sad that the spare camera had to become parts for its fellow cameras.

There have been plenty of times when reporters get in a hurry to get to a story or rush to get back to get to the TV station to meet a deadline. Some of those times have ended in a fender-bender or a news vehicle having to be totaled out. I was running late to work, as it happens from time to time, and got a call from my news director.

"Sweets, how far away are you from work?" he asked.

"Not too far," I replied.

"Well, I need you to go by and pick up Raven and take her to have a drug test. She's been in an accident."

Raven is a photographer.

"Okay, no problem," I said.

I was actually not too far from where the accident happened. I get there and things had been cleared out. She was waiting. Apparently, the car was not drivable and had to be towed away.

"Are you okay, Raven?" I asked.

"I'm okay," she responded.

"They asked for me to come get you and take you to the clinic to get a drug test."

"Okay, that's fine."

"So, what happened?"

"I'm really not sure. It happened so fast."

I'm thinking *that's right. Stick to giving as few details as possible.* She had been in a couple of weird incidents in the parking lot at work where she hit some other company vehicles. Nothing was done. Guess you can't file a claim against yourself. Now this! This may be it! Some people at work think she is a little odd. She kind of is. She's nice, though. She's very earthy and green before being green became cool.

I heard she had made our news director really mad one day. He is a heavy smoker. Has been for years. He had his chest cracked open some years back for double bypass surgery, and he still smoked. He went to take a smoke break one day and couldn't find his new pack of cigarettes, minus two he had smoked earlier. He searched high and low, asking every so often if anyone had seen them. Finally, Raven told some folks, including Vanessa Pacheco, one of our anchors, what she had done with them, and in doing so, she had banged up the package they were in pretty good. Vanessa couldn't believe she did that to someone's property even though she didn't smoke. It looked like the cigarettes may have all been bent and broken up. Eventually, Raven left the pack of cigs in the anchor's dressing room where the news director found them. He was livid.

"Who in the hell did this shit?" he asked. "I'm a grown ass

man!"

By this time, just about everybody knew what was going on. Natalie mentioned it to Robin, Galean, Elictia, Kevin, Taylor, Bob, Brad, Allysa, Ashleigh, Courtney Ann, Quinn, and Quentis. Quentis told Dwayne, Kiera, Tim, Tina, Frankie, Dorie, Billy, Branson, Jonnie, Damien, Michael Perry, Candace, Courtney, Cindy, Vicki, Judy, Gwen, Celia, JennyLeigh, Deidra, Robert, Rick, Audra, Zack, Nathan, Ben, Drew, Yolanda, Renee, Patrice, Veronica, Elizabeth, Jessica, Layla, Kelly, Jubal, Sharon, Denise, Marchant, Erica, Eric and Erik, Melissa, Jac, Blair, Scott, Matt, Austin, Leah, Luke, Steve, Keith, and Marva. She told John, Misty, Tammy, Darrell, Nicoli, Katie, Mike, Tre, Lori and Erin. Who told Anthony, Pam, Heather, Khara, Tiffany, Mark, Lynn, Jenna, and Margaret Ann. She told Louis, Ted, Wil, Dan, Jerome, Brian, Cory, J.P., Tiffany, Ryan, Glen, and Kensley. He told Stephen and Doug, plus Nick, Rex, and Patrick, the weather guys, Ashlea, Briar, Alexis, Chelsea, Lee, Brandon, Chessa, Charles, Drew, Dubbie, Mickey, Jonathan, Daniel, Tory, Thomas, Jim, Lauren, Shelby, AJ, Amanda, Adam, Ron, J.T., Mercer, Travis, Jordan, Jayson, and Mon. Eddie found out, too. Jennifer told him. As you can see, mess travels fast around the station. Everyone finds out, sooner or later. Eddie was the nearest person in front of the news director, and he came clean, ASAP. He was a former smoker, so he understood both sides. Lucky for Raven, she had left for a story. Our news director had the chance to calm down and smoke one of his bent cigarettes. He didn't see Raven until the next day. He had let it go and never said anything to her about it, but she was told how he went out of his mind about what she did.

She seemed a little unsettled on the drive to the clinic. I guess rightly so after the accident and thinking back on the news director's rant about her green-living and destroying his pack of cigs. She is probably thinking *this is it*. She passed the drug test and, although the accident was her fault and the news vehicle was totaled, she kept her job.

That wasn't the end of news vehicles being involved in questionable circumstances. Russell Brewer, he was a sports anchor/reporter. Sports people were the worst on news vehicles for some reason. Whenever new cars were added to the fleet, sports never got one but got a used news vehicle that was still in fair condition. This particular day was clear skies and beautiful. Russell had been acting agitated all day. He managed to get himself somewhat together to go to his shoot. Before he could get back, the receptionist transferred a call to management. Shortly, we would all know what that call was about.

"Goddammit!" The news director said, as he came screaming out of his office.

He has a hard time holding it in.

"I just don't understand that damn sports department," He goes on.

He feels comfortable talking freely because the whole sports department, including the sports director, is out covering stories. It's signing day in the South. It is crazy from sunup to sundown for the sports department. They are run ragged.

"Some lady just called to say a news vehicle just ran her off the road, and she wants something done about it."

Now, you can spot our vehicles a mile away, of course. We have every kind of way for you to log on and keep up with what's going on in the Pine Belt wrapped around every inch of those vehicles, including our network affiliation logos. There is no mistaking a news vehicle for anything else but a news vehicle. Why would you run someone off the road? Plus, sports had the only baby blue vehicle in the fleet, so it was easy to figure out who it was after the lady gave the description. Obviously, this is not the sports department's first time running into a little offense and having to come up with a defensive plan. They've had speeding tickets, their vehicles towed because they were in a hurry and parked in a fire zone, running out of gas and not getting regular oil changes, causing the engine to shut down. Oh, don't let me forget to mention a sports employee letting her boyfriend drive the sports car somewhere without her even being in it with him. Did I mention he was a known drug dealer?

"I'm sick of this shit! Who's driving the blue sports car?" he asked.

In unison, the majority of the folks in the newsroom said, "Russell."

"His ass is suspended from driving a station vehicle," he said as he returns to his office, and employees grab their cell phones to spread the word.

Now, not all station vehicles are involved in accidents. No, no, no. They are also used for a quickie. I'm happy to provide you with some clarity.

Our receptionist is kept quite busy with crazy phone calls from regular day-to-day business at the TV station. So the flood of phone calls she receives about the staff just blend on in. It took the masses a while to find out about the latest complaint, but everyone in the station eventually did, days later. Trust me, that's a long time. News people can't hold a thing. It's good as told. Come on, that's what we get paid to do. Professional life blends in with real life. It can't be stopped. News people are only human, too. This complaint, I must say, shocked me. That's pretty hard to do. I've been at the TV news game for a while.

Jacob Miller, he was a news photographer. Yeah, we had those, before corporate saw dollar signs with the switch to one-man bands. Now, our reporters have to shoot for themselves. We miss so much that way. You know, reporters setting up their own camera to shoot their stand-up while they miss filming the real crazy story going on behind them. The money shot, gone. Anyways, I guess Jacob had some time before his next shoot and decided to go somewhere else first. There is an area about a quarter mile up from the station we call the *beach resort* for the locals. No, we don't work by the ocean. It's a river that has a man-made bank that residents spruced up into a simulation of a resort. It's surrounded by a heavily-wooded area. People hang out there all day and all night cooking out, tanning, kids run around playing. They swim in that brown water like it's a luxurious chlorine-filled five-star pool at the Bellagio. Jacob decided he would take a break at the river resort and so did our viewer who called into the station. She decided to hit up the same spot Jacob decided to hit up. Unbeknownst to her, her spot was taken. She pulled up to a naked ass-crack against the window of a news vehicle that was violently rocking back and forth. Damn! Somebody was having sex in the professional-use-only news vehicle. She immediately put her car in reverse, as the two resort lovebirds stopped to see her pulling off. What ensued the call to the receptionist and the trickle down of information to the masses. Once the word started getting out, folks couldn't believe it! The questions came flooding in. How did he think that was a good idea in broad daylight? Who was he having sex with? His wife? No, I thought. She works, too, at that same time of day. She

Broadcast, Bloopers & Boneheads

was eliminated from the speculation shortly. Terrica got back from physical therapy, unaware of what was going on. She had been in an accident up the street last week. Her car was totaled, but she was alive. Thank God! I don't know what I would have done if the accident had been worse! She is my ride or die! My partner-in-crime! I'm making it sound more exciting than it is. She and I don't do much. Just terrorize some folks on the production staff. They deserve it! Anyways, she was quickly brought up to speed. And we quickly found out that it wasn't Jacob's wife he was having fun with at the resort on his lunch break quickie. Jacob's wife works where Terrica gets her physical therapy. Yep! She was at work today. Well, now, the story has a new layer and has escalated to ultra-juicy! Jacob got back in from the story he finally got around to shooting, and was quickly called in the office with management, and at that point, employees with their cellphones in their hands amped up to a hundred percent. Poor guy, I guess. Well, whatever happened wasn't enough to get him fired or suspended. He was back the next day, embarrassed to his core, and I'm sure glad nobody knew his wife really well, so maybe she won't find out. Over the next few weeks, anytime Terrica needed a photographer to go anywhere, Jacob volunteered. He brought her lunch at least once a week from her favorite wing joint for a good while. She accepted graciously. What else was she supposed to do? She really couldn't say, "Jacob why are you buying me lunch all the time?"

In weeks to come, it was back to business as usual. Stuff breaking, engineering fixing it, news vehicles needing to be maintained and detailed. Boy, if the detail crew only knew what had happened in Jacobs' news vehicle. I mean, the station's contracted car cleaning service is not scrubbing for bodily fluids. They are just trying to remove dirt and the food crumbs folks have left behind. Would you have sex on the cloth seats in your vehicle? I wouldn't think so, unless you are a teenager, let me add, who shouldn't be having sex. But it happens, folks. Or if you are a college student, age eighteen to twenty-two, who lives in a dorm. After that age, circumstances end for having sex in a vehicle.

12.
Using the airwaves to get a date, while others don't go far to have an affair

DO YOU THINK coworkers should date? Who am I kidding? So, should coworkers have sex with each other? Whether you think they should or shouldn't, they do, especially coworkers in TV news. Why is this? I'm not sure, but I have a few theories. A lot of young people work in TV news. Most come straight out of college, they are a cheap workforce. They want to live the dream, no matter how fuzzy it is. And unsurprisingly, this is the most sexually active age group there is. Put them around each other and they can't control themselves. I guess it's the beautiful people syndrome. TV news can have long work hours, so you're around each other a lot. You go to lunch together sometimes, ride to stories together all the time, and even hang out outside of work from time to time. You kind of get consumed with each other. It goes without saying that when you are twenty-something and hot, that leads to sex. And it can extend to the folks you interview in the public, sometimes. I have examples of all these scenarios. Just hold on.

Now, the newcomers who come from out-of-state seem to be the worst. Since they are not from here, they don't care about the locals knowing their business. Three or four weeks in on the job and you can tell who the horny ones are, and lack-of-having-sex ones, too - or prudes. They are ready to give it up to the first person lying down. Then, there are the ones that don't live so far from home. You know, at most, they live a couple of states over and can get home to get *some* on their off-days. Then you have those that live far away, and have to slum the bars and clubs, and go home with the ones who recognize them from being on TV. That's the no-fail plan right there!

There are all kinds of ways to get the job done. I thought I had seen it all, but there's always someone that comes along and stands out, and becomes one of the station's legends you talk about for years to come. This one person I'm talking about comes by way of California. Surely, the South was a culture shock as soon as he signed his lease. He's the newest addition to the three-man sports department. Ken Newton comes from a background of professional athletes. His dad is a former professional boxer. His brother is an MVP and former NFL player. To me, Ken really didn't have the California curse. You know, everybody wanting to be a celebrity, or live the lifestyle. But he had his own personality out right. Some folks thought he was a bit arrogant. I didn't pay him any attention. I put him in check one time and moved right along. I had no more problems. We became cool friends. Despite his incredible knowledge of sports, he always seemed nervous on air. For some news folks new to live TV, being in front of that camera gets them every time. Eventually, he got better.

One night in particular, Ken decided to let his personality shine. It had been a slow day for sports. Late summer doesn't provide much local sports news. Anticipation of the high school football season as well as the first NFL pre-season game is the best you are going to get.

Ken was done early with his sportscast, so he was lounging around the newsroom asking, "Where are all the news interns?"

"At home," I said. "Sit your horny butt down somewhere. I can see it all in your body language."

"Tam, don't act like that. I'm not getting *any* here, yet, and I need *some* girl," he laughed.

"Well, you need to be a little more discreet," I suggested.

"I am discreet. I have my eye on one intern in particular, ok?"

I find it incredible how the incoming class of interns each semester becomes the "dating pool" for wed and unwed TV station employees.

"Oh, so just one, you say?" I reiterated.

"Yes, Tam for now. If she doesn't act right, I'll go to one

more," he said, as he laughed out loud again. "I'm going to do my best to take them one at a time."

"What do you mean by one at a time, joker?" I asked.

"That means I'm not going to sleep with two interns at the same time. I'm going to pace myself," he explained.

Wow - the beautiful people! This semester we have quite a few interns, and they are all pretty good looking. This is an exceptional group of interns, talent-wise. They are knowledgeable about the news-gathering process, and they are very competitive already! And most of all, they are hardworking. To have all these qualities in one group like this is extremely rare. They all want a job after graduation, of course, but we only have a couple of spots that may come available. Let the cutthroat internship begin.

Well, time is winding down to show time. So far, we have no breaking news. Ken is in his sports office. I'm sure he's plotting his strategy for when he gets in tomorrow, which happens to be peak time for interns in the newsroom. So, I, along with my 10 o'clock anchor, Dana Quesenberry, who I love to death, head toward the studio. My other anchor for my 10 o'clock show, Steven Williams, is on vacation. He is in my circle, too. I think the world of him! Over the years, he always took the time to answer any question I had. He knows everything! He's like a walking Internet. He helped me become a better writer. I understand politics better because of him. That's not my favorite subject, but I became more interested because of him. Yes, it is something to bring attention to. Behind-the-scenes people, like myself, get along great with the on-air talent. Well, some on-air talent. Plus, they are my good friends outside of work. Anyway, Steve travels out of the country to the best places all the time. This time, he's traveled to South Africa. I can't wait to hear about his trip! I hope to travel like that someday, too!

Dana and I stopped by the lounge really quickly. She got some water, and I microwaved my tea from earlier. She headed to the news set, and I headed to the control room. The show open rolled, and we are on the air. The first block of news went well, except for when the Chyron operator hurriedly tried to prevent a mistake on a graphic from going on live TV. The Chyron op typed shit instead of shot on a graphic. The mistake was taken down fast, but I'm sure somebody took a *screenshot* of it and put it on our Facebook page. Now, we are in a commercial break. My director, Alphonzo, told me the camera operator said Dana needed me in the studio. I walked into the studio.

"What's up Q?" I said.

"Girl, I don't know why I'm so thirsty. Will you go get me some more water, please?" she asked.

I told her, "No problem."

I was back in a flash, just before the commercial spot ended. The public would be surprised to know what goes on during commercial breaks during a live newscast. Getting water is nothing to write about, but what happened in the commercial break before the sports block that night is!

We got through the second news block and commercial break. Weather comes next, and then we go to another commercial break. This is the break right before sports. It's kind of a short break. Ken comes to the studio and gives us a mic check. Mic check is good.

I give him an IFB check and after yelling at the director, he yelled at the camera operator, who then told Ken, "I don't think you have an IFB in."

Ken ran off the set to his desk to get his IFB. My only way to communicate with talent during the show is to talk to them through their IFB they put in their ear. Please bring it to the set with you, people! Anyways, Ken barely made it back to the set before the sports open-rolled, and Zo, a.k.a Alphonzo, punched him up on air. Wilhemina, who is my 6 p.m. show director, is on audio, going off.

"I get so tired of him forgetting that damn IFB all the time," she said.

I think Mina yelled some more expletives, but I was so focused on what camera shot we were going to next that I didn't hear her clearly. I didn't know if we were coming to an empty chair, or to Dana, who- would look like a deer in headlights. Zo popped Ken up on air. Ken didn't miss a beat, and sports, is over. We go to break. To the public, the show looked flawless, so to myself I'm like *forget saying anything.* I'm tired and ready to go home. Let's just get this over with. Not so fast- I'm absolutely floored by what happened before we ended the show.

During our last commercial break, unbeknownst to me until Dana told me play-by-play after the show was over, Ken had a piece of paper with his cell number written very large on it. Huh? I'm thinking *why?*

She said she noticed it and asked him, "Why do you have your number written on that piece of paper?"

"I'm thinking about holding it up for the camera at the end of the show," he replied.

"Are you crazy?" she asked. "You can't give your cell number out like that on live TV!"

It really wasn't his cell number. It was his work cell phone number. But still!

"I'm doing it as a fun way to get a date. I'm sure a girl is going to call me," he confidently said.

Dana spent the three-minute break trying to talk this joker out of doing this craziness. Well, she failed. Without time to say much more than good night at the close of the show, Ken managed to get his number up in time. We were horrified. When I went back to look at the close of the show, his number was up for seven seconds- long enough for someone to screenshot it, write it down, freeze the DVR, tweet it, and re-tweet it! What was he thinking- that some girls would really call? Well, they did. He is quite handsome. And I'm sure he had plenty of time to take some of them out during his three-day suspension. The stuff I've had to go through in this business!

Not everyone gets suspended, though. Some folks have had their affairs with other co-workers in the workplace and manage to not get suspended. How is that? I don't know. But I can tell you what happened.

Our main weather anchor, Ines Ingram, is beautiful. Who doesn't want a little eye candy? Forecasting the weather can sometimes be boring. She started out as an intern and worked her way up. That's an easier process for some than others in the news business when you have certain assets, if you know what I mean.

Then there is Jason Spilner. He and Ines both started out as interns together. He's now a reporter. He's not the best we got. But we had to find him something to do that he couldn't get wrong. He does franchise stories. His main one is Tax Tip Tuesday. Ines also reports once a week. Her story is always weather-related. They both sit across from each other in the newsroom. She not only has her weather office in the back but also has a news desk in here with us. We can remember them flirting with each other since their internships. Who doesn't flirt? But, over the years, it progressed. Gradually, but we noticed the whole way. We are news people. That's what we do. Notice everything. If you come into this business lacking in that area, you will quickly catch up if you want to keep up. You would think since we are in the communications business that we are in constant communication with one another. Nope. I constantly have to overhear conversations in the newsroom in order to know what's going on. Why? Surely, being the producer, I shouldn't have to work this hard at newsgathering. Because as soon as the first mistake happens, whether it was my fault or not, I'm the one blamed.

Well, years of flirting developed into lunch dates. What coworkers don't go to lunch with each other? Right? No big deal. We show up to coworker gatherings outside of work without spouses, or partners all the time. Sometimes we news people all together in one spot are too much for spouses, girlfriends and boyfriends.

Now, at this point both are married. Ines was the last one to get married. Jason brought his pregnant wife to her wedding. Hmm. Men are stupid. I had to explain their relationship to the sales manager one day at one of my favorite boutiques where I shop. One day before going to work, Terrica and I met there on her lunch break. The manager, Syrenthia, knows us well and proceeded to ask us,

"Do Ines and Jason date? They come in here quite often together. They seem to get along with each other very well," she said.

Terrica and I made eye contact and smiled.

I said, "No they are not dating. They are married to other people."

The look on her face when I said that!

What's the saying? All good things must come to an end. That day came with a bang one night for us in the newsroom.

Let me give you a little backstory here:

I was out of town at All-Star weekend in Houston, so I missed the party at Kesha's. I think it was a co-worker's birthday party or something. Trust me. That's not important. Well, attraction, plus a little liquor among coworkers, equals a disappearance before the night is over. Jason and Ines come back, disheveled. People noticed. However, they didn't. Next, Ines was sitting in Jason's lap. Again, people noticed. They didn't. What happened in the days to come led me to believe that someone told Jason's wife about this. Who that was, I still can't figure out to this day. We'd managed to keep it the elephant-in-the-room all that time.

I'm in my six o'clock show one night, and the phone rang by the producer's desk. I'm now aggravated that someone is calling me during the show. My live shots are over!

I picked up the phone and, aggressively, said, "Hello?"

No one said anything. Now, I'm really hot. I look at the caller I.D. and realize it's one number off from Jason's cell number.

So I go, "Hanna?"

That's Jason's wife's name.

She goes, "Tam?"

"Hey, girl, what's up?" I say hurriedly, and wondering *why is she calling this number?*

Plus, Jason was off today. He called in sick, so I thought. I'm trying to time a show here.

"I've found out about Jason and Ines's affair."

My brain was delayed, trying to tell myself, *girl did you hear what she just said?*

If you could have seen my face, I felt so vulnerable.

I could only manage, "Oh?"

She proceeds to tell me they had it out, and he finally told her about the affair that's being going on for a couple of months. I'm thinking *ohhhh? Okay! It's been longer than that!* That's all I can remember. Well, that's all I'm going to say. I've never been put in the middle of some mess like that. Let alone a co-worker's mess! I felt so violated. Not only have I had to brunt the public's questions when they asked about Ines and Jason, I had to be sucked in, involuntarily, because I answered the work phone.

Apparently, she was calling back numbers in his cell phone and reached this one. I don't blame her. I would have probably done the same thing. Poor thing, *I thought. She's about to be a single parent.*

The affair spread like wildfire into the community from the hills to the hood. My favorite monogram shop became a holding room for me. The owner was Hanna's friend and knew I worked at the station. I got V.I.P. treatment and was taken to the back of the store to pick out whatever I wanted in this super nice room, in exchange for telling how the co-worker's acted around each other at work. Wasn't really much to say, you know. We didn't see them even speak to each other in the newsroom for weeks.

Well, somehow Ines's husband found out, too. A couple of months went by, with the biggest neon-elephant in the room. Ines and Jason sat across from one another and rarely ever talked to each other.

Then, one night, it all went down!

I guess Ines and her husband were trying to bond more, and rebuild their marriage. It looked like she had no intention of leaving her marriage. He came back with her to work one night. I believe they had gone to dinner together. Ines worked nights, so I could see how it was difficult for them to spend time together. Looked like they were making an effort. Jason was gone for the day, so no chance of the two menfolk running into each other.

Wrong! Jason was in the building, unbeknownst to the rest of us. He forgot something and came back to get it. The night crew started coming back in from their dinner breaks. The crew was coming and going. Jason came in to the newsroom. We were like *oh, shit!* You could see it on all of our faces. We were looking around for Ines's husband. We didn't see him. Ines hadn't noticed Jason in the newsroom until right then. Oh, damn! That was the look on her face. We didn't know what to do. We all looked up, it was like slow motion, and there came Ines's husband. The menfolk were face-to-face for what we all were thinking was the first time since it all went down. We were right. We couldn't look away. Then, they made eye contact. I was about to faint but couldn't because what came next was a Louisiana ass-whooping, front and center, in full color, HD, seventy-two-inch screen, real time...okay, you get it. I guess his emotions got the best of him coming face-to-face with his wife's ex-lover. He lunged at Jason, and his first punch landed on his target hard. You could hear all of us suck the air out of the room. The fight was one-sided, folks. That Louisiana boy whooped Tax Tip Tuesday's ass! Some of the guys tried to pull him off, but, even collectively, they couldn't. He wasn't that big of a guy but he was tall, about 6'2", and quick with this hands, and stronger than I imagined. And the bees came stinging from all around on Jason's 5'8" frame. Ines was hollering and screaming. I was trying to keep her from getting too close and getting knocked out because her man wasn't seeing anybody but the man who had sex with his wife. There was nothing we could do but watch a straight ass-whooping. Thank God, by this time Zo came back from his break. He's half-man, half-diesel. He's 6'5" of muscle. Jason would live to see another day. Zo easily grabbed Ines's man off of Jason's battered body. Under any other circumstances, we would have called the sheriff, but we couldn't. This was a family matter. You could see it on our faces that we felt like *oh well*. Plus, we had a newscast to get on. And, besides, we couldn't let this drama get out for other media outlets to find out about. The only people who like to share information more than media professionals are the local law enforcement. Silently, we made a pact not to even tell management. Not a word to them about what happened. We felt like Ines's husband evened the score. We were glad for him. We think he got some needed closure. Good for him. It was only fair.

Jason came to work the next day with his on-air HD makeup already on. You could tell he was covering up some bruising. I bet he had ice packs all over his body last night, to keep down the swelling with pain meds on the nightstand. It is like Las Vegas around here for the elephant in the room. He constantly has a residency.

In years to come, I heard privellage pushed Jason right on up the corporate ladder and he was in management at a newsroom somewhere. Wow! Some folks get it so easily. They are given their work history and don't have to be the best to get promoted. I can only imagine the news judgment and moral compass in that station's newsroom.

www.ingramcontent.com/pod-product-compliance
Lightning Source LLC
Chambersburg PA
CBHW070055120526
44588CB00033B/1442